EVERYTHING
IS A
F*CKING
STORY

A PREQUEL TO THE HABIT FACTOR®
AND THE PRESSURE PARADOX™

RECOGNIZE AND
REWRITE THE STORIES
THAT *STEER* YOUR LIFE

#EaFStory #TrueStory

MARTIN GRUNBURG

EQUILIBRIUM ENTERPRISES, INC.

Library of Congress Cataloging-in-Publication data is available upon request.
ISBN: 978-0982050194
Grunburg, Martin A.
Everything is a F*cking Story – *Recognize & Rewrite the Stories that Steer your Life*

First Edition: October 2022
Printed in the United States

Praise for
EVERYTHING!

"This book shows you how to overcome hidden thoughts and beliefs that may have held you back decades...don't be surprised if you feel liberated overnight!"

⚓

Brian Tracy, personal development legend,
author of over 70 books

"Grunburg's 'Three Circles' behavior model is paradigm-shifting. It's helped to transform our executive coaching. Because of 'Everything,' we teach, coach, and train: 'Change your story, change your habits, change your life.'"

⚓

Dr. Peter Chee, CEO and founder of ITD World,
author of *Coaching for Breakthrough Success*

"*Powerful! As founder of the world's largest entrepreneurial organization (EO), a recurring theme – a pattern – reveals itself among the most successful entrepreneurs: They have the habit of driving a hopeful, positive narrative – a compelling STORY – not just for their companies but for their lives, families, and in many cases, their communities. Every entrepreneur's journey begins and ends right here!*"

⚓

Verne Harnish, author of stories, CEO of Scaling Up

"*A profound personal development trilogy – read this book! At myNeuroGym.com, we've taught for well over a decade that when you want to improve your results in any area of your life, the very first place to begin is your thinking! Martin's work with 'Everything' makes that singular message reverberate so loudly and clearly that you'll find yourself assessing your own stories, constantly, in all areas of your life.*

⚓

John Assaraf, New York Times bestselling author,
Having it All* and *The Answer

"Martin may be the best-kept secret in the world of behavior change. His work on habit is intuitive, practical, and impactful. In this book, he correctly highlights our natural drive for storytelling and how we can direct the stories we tell ourselves. This change in narrative is at the heart of personal transformation. Grunburg's approachable prose and flow show much wisdom and is straightforward to apply. I hope more people learn about these ideas and about Martin in the coming years!"

⚓

Glenn R. Fox, Ph.D., Neuroscientist & Professor
USC Marshall School of Business

"In a sea of regurgitated personal development ideas, Grunburg's work is refreshingly out-of-the-box and filled with powerful insights!"

⚓

Kevin Daum, Inc. 500 entrepreneur,
six-time bestselling author, Inc. columnist

"Positively life-changing! As a 15x Ironman, along with being a CEO coach and professional sales trainer, having now taught hundreds of thousands of business professionals worldwide, I've never met a successful professional who didn't first construct a powerful, personal STORY. 'Everything' is exceedingly discerning in revealing how it is that narrative permeates every aspect of our life. Read this book—reap the rewards!"

⚓

Jack Daly, 15-time Ironman, three-time number-one Amazon bestselling author, CEO coach

"We coach hundreds of the top entrepreneurs and CEOs from some of the world's finest companies, and the beginning of 'success' – the key to making BIG happen – is to start with an empowering, supportive story. Grunburg's work here is excellent in directing the reader to grasp this first, powerful truth! Read this, study this – a great personal development trilogy for every aspiring professional and entrepreneur!"

⚓

Mark Moses, CEO & founding partner of Coaching International, bestselling author of *Make BIG Happen*, 12-time Ironman, business coach to some of the world's top entrepreneurs and CEOs

"In deceptively simple language, Martin yet again hits the nail of metaphysical reality squarely on the head. Many of our current human stories are creating misery, depression, division, and conflict. Martin's timely reminder that it's all story, and stories can be changed, gives us an escape hatch from our current predicament and points toward a world of greater happiness, fulfillment, tolerance, and harmony. Prepare to see through fresh eyes and transform your future!"

⚓

Dr. Rosalind Savage, MBE,
author, speaker, ocean rower

"If you want to predict your future SUCCESS, you must look closely at your daily habits. One habit that most people never stop to think about is the habitual stories they tell themselves about life. 'Everything' will help you become instantly aware of all your stories and the profound effects they have on your SUCCESS."

⚓

Jairek Robbins, president of SUCCESS Enterprises

"As a behavioral scientist and management consultant for more than 20 years, this book, 'Everything,' shines a powerful spotlight on aspects of our thinking critical to our success – STORY as 'Thought 2.0' – a powerful concept that has real and far-reaching impact and effect on our personal and professional life – our future!"

⚓

Holly G. Green, CEO and managing director of The Human Factor, Inc., Thinking to Thrive expert, global management consultant, award-winning speaker, bestselling author

"Martin nails it! As a successful entrepreneur and executive coach, I know change begins at one's roots – their stories. From one's identity, various narratives flow, forming their values, possibilities, decisions, actions, and habits. This lesson alone cannot be overvalued. Put these lessons in action now, and see how EVERYTHING comes together to improve your RESULTS!"

⚓

Tony Lillios, personal and professional coach

"You want to accelerate your company's results? Get your STORY straight! Ensure you have a vision – a story – that is clearly articulated and aligned with your behaviors and habits. This is how you will produce a winning company culture!"

⚓

Cameron Herold, founder and COO of Alliance, author of *Double Double*

"Less expensive and a lot more fun than therapy, this is a delightful read. I don't know about you, but too much self-analysis makes me want to take a nap. A good story? I always have one. I had read The Habit Factor, and this is a wonderful complement to his insights about how we operate as humans. In this case...how we stall our own progress. Thanks for making self-discovery easier and more fun."

⚓

Timi Gleason, executive and leadership coach, founder of Soulworkmaps.com

"Authors do not choose the story to
write; the story chooses us."
~Richard P. Denney

This book is dedicated to my beautiful,
uniquely gifted, and slightly eccentric parents,
married 54 years and counting...

Eternal Love and Gratitude! ∞

"God made man because He loves stories."

~Elie Wiesel

"That's what we storytellers do. We restore order with imagination. We instill hope again and again and again."

~Walt Disney

"Once upon a time..."

When Banzan was walking through a market, he overheard a conversation between a butcher and his customer.

"Give me the best piece of meat you have," said the customer.

"Everything in my shop is the best," replied the butcher. "You cannot find here any piece of meat that is not the best."

At these words, Banzan became enlightened.

TABLE OF CONTENTS

CONTENTS

FOREWORD

By Rick Sessinghaus, Psy.D, PGA

PGA Championship Coach

Ambassador TaylorMade Golf Company, Brand Ambassador Adidas Golf,
NLP Certified Master Trainer

I recall well the day I first tripped upon The Habit Factor. It was early 2012; I had just boarded my Southwest flight and was thumbing through the inflight magazine, *SPIRIT*. A review article about New Year's resolutions and goal achievement, featuring tools and strategies, caught my attention.

As a professional golf coach working with both amateur and professional PGA players, my specialty focus is on the "mental game." The more I learned about The Habit Factor, the more intrigued I became.

The in-flight feature positioned The Habit Factor in a unique light; it was the first time I'd noticed any book about goal achievement with a corresponding mobile app – a way for readers to implement the book's principles – to put them into *practice*.

Further, it was the first time, in all the years of my professional study and practice, in which the pathway to goal achievement was articulated in such simple terms. Rather than a series of "steps" or following a "best practice," like S.M.A.R.T. goals, The Habit Factor method simply involved identifying core, related behaviors – habits – that one could intentionally craft and align to their goals.

I was so interested to learn more that before we even took flight, I downloaded the book's Kindle version; by the time the plane landed, I had nearly finished reading it.

At the time, I had a handful of students who, despite our best efforts, were not progressing as quickly as we'd hoped. As a professional coach, such situations are perplexing. I was confident in the lessons and guidance I offered; however, the actual results – the improvement – we expected to see was not materializing.

After reading The Habit Factor, I recognized how I could apply its principles to my students. I dove headfirst into The Habit Factor method, feeling this could be the tool and process to connect the "mental game" to the athlete's on-course performance.

A few months after that Southwest flight, I reached out to the author to inquire about The Habit Factor Certified Professionals Program.

By then, I'd already put many of its ideas into practice and was excited and encouraged about how it was helping my athletes.

I sent the following to Martin:

Sent: Monday, May 07, 2012 12:25 PM
Subject: RE: The Habit Factor Certified Professional Program

Hi Martin,
Looking forward to becoming certified in The Habit Factor. I have thoroughly enjoyed the book and have already implemented the strategies into my coaching…I believe The

Habit Factor complements my coaching philosophy, and with the app, it helps me in implementing training behaviors (habits) for my clients.

I am very interested in bringing The Habit Factor to the corporate arena, as well.

Thank you and looking forward to learning more from you.

Sincerely,

Rick Sessinghaus Psy.D

"Golf's Mental Coach"

Author of Golf: The Ultimate Mind Game

Fundamentally, the shift was substantial as my athletes began to focus their attention on developing the core, related, and foundational habits needed to reach their goals; we tracked and monitored their progress.

For example, there was Robert W., an amateur golfer who appeared stuck at a scoring plateau. We applied the basic habit-tracking principles following The Habit Factor's P.A.R.R. (Plan, Act, Record, and Reassess) methodology, focusing our attention specifically toward the habits surrounding his tournament preparation.

The premise was his enhanced concentration upon preparation would result in better scoring. We identified just three habits to track: 1) a minimum of eight hours of sleep before rounds, 2) just five minutes of devoted mindfulness once at the course, and 3) reviewing the strategy as we headed into each round.

We would Plan, Act, Record, and Reassess (P.A.R.R.), and we would review our "actuals," what actually happened, against our "targets," what we planned to happen.

In a relatively short period of time, about six months, the results were unmistakable. Robert transformed from being anxious and even at times jittery to becoming far calmer and more confident as he headed into each round.

By simply putting our attention upon a specific preparation routine, Robert cultivated a series of habits in relatively short order that lowered, on average, his tournament round scores by two shots – a significant breakthrough at this level!

A few years later, around 2015, Martin shared with me his new, soon-to-be-released book, *The Pressure Paradox*. This book reaffirmed my position, based upon years of teaching and experience as a professional competitor, that pressure could be a tremendous asset – an aid to athletes – to help them to perform at higher levels once they had planned, prepared, and practiced appropriately.

Here again, Martin took an "outside-the-box" alternative viewpoint; first, it was with habits and now with pressure. And, once again, his thesis flew contrary to so many experts and coaches within the performance arena who insist that pressure is "bad," "evil," or even a "nemesis to one's success." His work with *The Pressure Paradox* is groundbreaking.

Now, to bring our backstory current, I recently reached out to Martin seeking some guidance for my new book and, in ending my email, asked if he might be working on any new projects.

I should have known better. It turns out, the answer to that question is what you are reading or listening to now.

Martin eagerly shared with me his working excerpt of this book, *Everything*. It is not only a fascinating read, but as a professional coach, it is spectacular. Once again, he seems to have hit the nail on the head. Now, as he describes it, his *trilogy* is complete: *The Habit Factor*, *The Pressure Paradox*, and now, *Everything*. And dare I say, it's a powerful framework for any coach, in any arena, including business, personal, and professional athletics.

Story <-> Habits <-> Environment

After reading *Everything*, its lessons – these concepts – hit me right between the eyes. Our thinking – which apparently comes in the form of story, most of the time – directly influences and guides our behaviors, which in turn helps to shape our results.

We can process all sorts of good, helpful information, instruction, and lessons, but if our self-narrative is unsupportive, weak, hopeless, or perhaps even destructive – not "aligned," as Martin puts it, goal achievement becomes a futile endeavor.

I'm confident each reader and listener will see more clearly where they may need to edit, rewrite, or perhaps even simply ditch the stories that aren't serving their interests, goals, and ideals.

We all learn from stories. My students learn from stories. My upcoming book, *The Round of Your Life*, is laden with stories.

Humans remember stories far more than facts; stories not only educate, but they also conjure up emotions, which in turn guide our attention, focus, and behavior.

When our stories are curated and crafted properly with intention, then backed with intentional habit and skill development, we not only facilitate our performance, but our lives in general.

I am delighted that you picked up *Everything*, and I'm more than confident it will help you to craft the necessary and important stories to steer you toward your best life, which, of course, is certain to be a story worth sharing.

Most sincerely,

Rick Sessinghaus Psy.D.
Golf's Mental Coach
RickSessinghaus.com

PREFACE

*"Life can only be understood backwards,
but it must be lived forwards."*
~Søren Kierkegaard

When I began writing *The Habit Factor* in 2005
(published in 2010),[1] it was impossible to foresee that this
book – a prequel – would materialize nearly 20 years and
approximately 900 pages later.

Should the expletive in the title offend you, I apologize.
As you might expect, there's a *story* behind why we're using
it, which you'll find in the Epilogue.

With *Everything* now complete, there are three books in
the rearview mirror. Taken as a whole, they complete a
"Personal Mastery" trilogy. Here's the punchline: It's a
trilogy I never knew existed! After nearly two decades of
writing, researching, and exploring human behavior,
Everything ends the journey (for now).

To quickly recap: *The Habit Factor* (2010) was the first to
present a simple, effective methodology for goal
achievement via intentional habit development and
alignment. *The Habit Factor* revealed that the most efficient
path toward achieving our most important goals is to focus
on core, recurring behaviors (habits) instead of one-off
"steps" or some endless to-do list.

At the time, *The Habit Factor* challenged every goal achievement "best practice." Its mission: to help dispose of habit's negative connotation, i.e., smoking, drinking, drugs, biting nails, etc., and the erroneous idea that to achieve your goals, "you must avoid habits." (Of course, they were only thinking about "bad habits.")

Similarly, *The Habit Factor* exposed the S.M.A.R.T. goals methodology – still a leading goal-achievement process, but one that fails to address the role of habit, instead concentrating exclusively on "next steps." You may have noticed there's no "H" in the S.M.A.R.T. acronym.

Before publishing *The Habit Factor*, we released its supplemental app in the iTunes marketplace (June 2009). The app provided the tool – a literal application – to help users apply The Habit Factor principles following P.A.R.R. (Plan, Act, Record, & Reassess). It quickly rose to become a top-five productivity app on three continents *simultaneously*.

Over a decade later, the impact of *The Habit Factor* (book and app) and its method is unmistakable across myriad industries, including self-help, fitness tech, weight loss, wellness, and more. There are now upwards of 100 habit-tracking apps and dozens of best-selling productivity books espousing The Habit Factor's basic principles.

The second book of this unforeseen trilogy, *The Pressure Paradox*, was published in 2015. It explored how our environment, particularly pressure, influences our behaviors and achievements. Without *pressure*, personal transformation is *impossible*.

Pressure is the essential force initiating change.

The Pressure Paradox demonstrated beyond a shadow of a doubt that pressure isn't "negative" or "positive." Instead, it's a neutral force essential to our growth, achievement, success, and positive transformation.

The idea of pressure as an essential requirement *for success* flew in the face of popular opinion. Authors and noted professionals at the time, including performance and psychology experts, posited – and even warned – that pressure is "evil" and a "nemesis" to one's success.

At the same time, *The Pressure Paradox* introduced a concept called the "3 Circles," represented by three concentric circles. In this book, the "3 Circles" evolves significantly into the *"3 Circles of Behavior Echo-System."*

As you will see, you are living *within* this behavior echo-system right now. Everyone is.

The *3 Circles of Behavior Echo-System* is a model and a framework that can help anyone realize their most important, long-term goals and achieve personal transformation more effectively and efficiently.

This new behavior model deviates significantly from prevalent behavior models (some of which are 40 and 50 years old). These older models represent human behavior in a "circular" and "linear" fashion.[1]

The 3 Circles of Behavior Echo-System illustrates how our thoughts, emotions, feelings, and behaviors ECHO – they *reverberate* and influence one another.

---

[1] More in "The Three Circles (The Redux)" chapter.

Importantly, each book within this trilogy comprises one of the concentric circles.

The *Inner* Circle: Thoughts (*Stories*), Book #3
The *Middle* Circle: Behaviors (*Habits*), Book #1
The *Outer* Circle: Environment[2] (*Pressure*), Book #2

It's all so clear to me – *now*.

In *Everything*, we arrive at the final, concentric circle – the heart of this behavior model and its *bullseye*. While it's the last "circle" in the trilogy, it's also the foremost inner circle, and it represents our *thinking*.

Everything is specifically about how we think and how we can think "better" and more effectively as we pursue our goals and ideals.

If there has been one constant – a theme that spans all my books – it is this: We must pursue our ideal future, and "success" is simply a daily effort toward that end. Nobody creates their "success" any faster than just one day at a time.

Thus, creating your ideal future, from one day to the next, *is* success. There hasn't been a person in history who has realized success any other way – doing the best they can, with what they have, more days than not.

The daily pursuit of our goals and ideals *is* the absolute best use of our limited energy and time. Not coincidentally,

---

[2] Pressure is an environmental component; however, it is just one aspect of environment as defined herein. For a complete definition, see the "Three Circles" chapter.

it's also the absolute best gift we can give ourselves and our loved ones.

Numerous studies validate that hypothesis, presenting the inverse data that universally, the greatest regret people have about their life is that they did not make the most of their time or opportunities. Simply put: They did not pursue their goals and ideals.[2]

If I knew long ago that this book was to complete a "Personal Mastery" trilogy, I would have begun here, with this project, the inner circle: Thinking as story.

Our thinking shapes our "universe." How we think is critical, as are the thousands of little stories we tell ourselves about ourselves, our friends, family, and the world at large.

These stories directly influence our emotions, decisions, actions, and behaviors, even what we "see." When repeated enough, both thoughts (stories) and behaviors crystalize into habits.

Our stories can influence and alter our environment. For instance, the teenager who, with the repeated story, "I want to become a soldier and join the Army," is very likely to find themselves enlisted. (But I'm getting way ahead of myself.)

There's a wonderful saying attributed to many great minds, from Lao Tzu to Buddha and even Emerson, and it's only slightly modified here. It's also recounted within *The Habit Factor* and sets the stage beautifully as a backdrop for this trilogy:

Choose your thoughts, for they become your *words*;

Choose your words, for they become your *actions*;
Choose your actions, for they become your *habits*;
Choose your habits, for they become your *character*;
Choose your character, for it becomes your *destiny*.[3]

In this book, we dare to enter the realm of thought and entertain the bizarre concept that our primary means of thinking, cognitive function, and analysis is STORY.

In so doing, we'll explore meta-cognition (thinking about thinking). For instance, what is it that frames our thoughts? Where does one thought end and another begin? Grammatically speaking, that would be defined as a sentence. Yet, humans don't think in simple sentences most of the time, do they? Often, we "script" or "frame" our thoughts, and that "framing" is elongated into snippets – imaginative narratives…STORY.

So, we'll inspect and dissect how story is woven within, around, and throughout our lives.

We'll discover how these stories – the ones we consistently tell ourselves – ultimately influence our outcomes and results.

Finally, we examine how these stories facilitate our dreams, goals, and achievements or tragically push them further away, making them seem impossible.

This work seeks to help those who suspect that with better application, they can affect, influence, and improve

---

[3] Modified slightly, replacing the word "watch" with choose. Choice is a way to demonstrate control.

their circumstances by directing their mind's power with intention.

This book is written for those who intuitively know that although it comes as "standard equipment" (and is free), the mind is priceless and the "most powerful, smallest, and largest thing in the universe," as the 16th Gyalwa Karmapa put it. If his statement is even close to accurate, and the mind is this powerful, not applying it with purpose, direction, and intention, to put it lightly, is foolish.

Consider this: We're all, in essence, driving around a massive earthmover – an all-powerful vehicle that can take us wherever we want to go while redefining and beautifying our landscape. Unfortunately, most of us aren't even touching the steering wheel.

That precise analogy originates from Earl Nightingale's 1957 audio recording, *The Strangest Secret* (which sold more than 1 million copies). Nightingale's thesis, backed by many great philosophers throughout the ages, was:

"We become what we think about."

Thus, it's our sole responsibility to control, direct, and steer our thoughts – the stories we consistently tell ourselves – intentionally toward our own worthwhile goals and ideals.

In his timeless classic, *As a Man Thinketh*, author James Allen emphasized the importance of controlling our mind due to the inextricable connection between the body and mind. He wrote, "If you would protect your body, guard your mind. If you would renew your body, beautify your mind. Thoughts of malice, envy, disappointment, despondency, rob the body of its health and grace."

The ancient Buddhist text, the Dhammapada, a collection of eternal "truths," counsels: "As irrigators lead water where they want, as archers make their arrows straight, as carpenters carve wood, the wise shape their minds."

Thus, the idea of controlling our thinking has been written about since time immemorial, ad infinitum. And to be clear, I don't mean to imply that I have cornered the market on "right thought."

The work you are about to read is simply my journey into exploring and identifying patterns at the intersection of thought and achievement – what works and what doesn't, like my efforts within *The Habit Factor* and *The Pressure Paradox*.

The question remains: What is effective when it comes to "right thinking"? How do we take control of our mind's steering wheel? Who is teaching us to drive this massive earthmover? If our thinking (as you will learn) happens (more often than not) in the form of *story* – imaginative narrative – then perhaps we should better understand *story* and its component parts.

I am not a psychiatrist or psychologist. I don't hold any fancy letters next to my name. I do bring nearly 20 years of passion and dedication to the fields of self-improvement and behavior modification and much experience working directly and indirectly with countless people worldwide.

Finally, I bring an outsider's perspective, which is essential and typically where breakthroughs arise – *outside* industries and academia. Thus, the overly used cliché, "It's time we start thinking outside the box."

Without an outsider's perspective, neither *The Habit Factor* nor *The Pressure Paradox* would exist, nor could they have so positively impacted so many lives worldwide.

It's worth sharing that professionals worldwide *within* various education and behavioral science fields employ, teach, and recommend the principles and ideas in these works.

> Message: Hi Martin,
> Firstly let me say that I love your app, and have recommended it to several of my clients (I'm a psychologist). What would make it even better is if it had a logging option for habits which take time. So if my goal is to do X minutes a day, the habit would have a start and stop button.for me to ensure that I complete my target amount. All the best, Jeremy

Now, please allow me to tell you a story.

~mg

PROLOGUE

THOUGHT 2.0

*"Until the lion learns how to write,
every story will glorify the hunter."
~African Proverb*

Wrapping up a business lunch (three-plus years into this effort), and, *as the story goes*, one of the top engineers at our company was struggling with a challenging client. There was a tech project that involved hundreds of hours of "discovery" work. He believed his work to be accurate, yet the client was second-guessing his efforts, adding to his doubt and unrest.

At the time of this meeting, we had a 20-plus-year working relationship, and it was a habit of ours to meet up at least once a month for lunch. Even though it was a large project, and the client was a law firm, I wasn't losing sleep over it since I knew Steve was technically brilliant.

As we headed for the door, I tried to reassure him that I thought the situation would work out just fine.

"Steve, really, just let it go...don't overthink this," I said. "It's just a story she [the client] keeps playing over and over in her head."

Without hesitation, half looking toward me over his shoulder, he responded, *"Isn't everything?"*

I chuckled at his question, which was more of a statement. We headed to our cars.

"Isn't everything?"

His words echoed in my head for a few hours, then days, weeks, and months.

Isn't everything?

Isn't everything a story? I kept repeating the question.

Is it possible to separate our lives from our stories?

It just so happens that story – imaginative narrative – is inextricable from your existence!

Heck, you are reading or listening to this story right now!

This may come as a surprise to you, as it did to me: We actually think in terms of story. But don't take my word for it. Consider the words of cognitive scientist Mark Turner:

"Narrative imagining – story – is the fundamental instrument of thought. Rational capacities depend upon it. [Storytelling] is our chief means of looking into the future, of predicting, of planning, and of explaining."

It's as though stories are "Thought 2.0." A cat may see a bird and think maybe "bird" or "food." Humans see a bird and think, "That's a beautiful bird. Wow! Those colors remind me of Fiji, and man, I can't wait to get back to Fiji! The smell of the air, the weather, the waves! What an unbelievable honeymoon we had!"[3]

The following experiment took place in 1944, orchestrated by psychologists Fritz Heider and Marianne Simmel. They asked 34 participants to watch a short animation (approximately 90 seconds) that involved two triangles and a circle (or disc) that moved around a stationary rectangle partially open on one side. Throughout the animation, the triangles and circle move toward each other and in and out of the rectangle.

In the first part of the experiment, the scientists asked the participants to describe what they observed.[4]

So, how do you think the participants responded?

Rather than describing what they saw – a few animated shapes moving around – they crafted a story, and some were extremely elaborate.

For instance, the two triangles became two men "fighting," and the circle represented a woman who was "desperately trying to escape." The participants' interpretations went further. One explained how the circle was "worried" and that the bigger triangle was a "bully" who was suspected to be "blinded by rage and frustration."

Just one participant out of 34 described the short animation for what it was: animated shapes moving around.

Worth repeating: The animation was simply a couple of triangles and a circle moving in, out, and around a partially opened rectangle.[4]

It turns out we (humans) do this often. And, by often, I mean almost always. We intuit and associate "things," connect dots, and imply meaning – here comes the painful part – whether it's accurate or not.

Story – personalized narrative – is so thoroughly ingrained and woven into our thought process that it IS our thought process.

We habitually interpret our observations, project our intentions, make predictions, and infer meaning by drawing upon our experiences and the thousands of stories we've stored in our subconscious.

That's no coincidence or wordplay, by the way.

We store stories.

This is precisely what Mark Turner means when he says, "[Story] is our chief means of predicting, planning, and explaining." In his book, *The Literary Mind: The Origins of Thought and Language,* Turner states[5]:

---

[4] In my executive training and coaching presentations, responses are nearly identical. In fact, that family script/story came from a participant in a recent presentation.

"Story is a basic principle of mind. Most of our experience, our knowledge, and our thinking is organized as stories. The mental scope of story is magnified by projection – one story helps us make sense of another."

There isn't another creature in the world, as far as we know, that holds such a unique ability.[6]

How often have you heard someone say, for instance, about any situation, "Oh, we've seen this movie (or play, or story) before – we know how this is gonna end!"

Or, "I'm no dummy; I can read between the lines."
Or, "Wait! There's more to the story."
Or, "Let's see if we can flip the script."
Or, "That's it; that's the end of the story!"
Or, "Long story short."
Or, "You better stick to the f*cking script!"
Or, "You better get your f*cking story straight!"
Or, "Maybe you shouldn't read too much into it."

Or, this little gem, just used in a meeting this morning: "Allow me to share the Reader's Digest version."

How about this one, courtesy of ESPN, the all-sports network: "It's going to be fascinating to see what storylines emerge this season."

The examples of story integration into our language and thought process are seemingly endless.

Think about metaphors, similes, analogies, and even hyperbolic language devices. What happens when we use such mechanisms?

Consider William Shakespeare's "All the world's a stage, and all the men and women merely players." This supports *Everything's* thesis unusually well.

Further, consider these statements:
They're playing chess while you're playing checkers.
Wasting time is like throwing money down the drain.
Their tears flowed down their face like a river.

Perhaps a better question is, "Why do we use such language apparatus? Why do these thought and language tools exist?"
Why!?
I'll tell you why. Allow me to cut straight to the chase:

That's how we (humans) f*cking think.

In a world that may appear absolutely senseless, cruel, chaotic, and meaningless at any given moment, story offers a sense of order and hope.

Recall Disney's weighty observation from the open: "That's what we storytellers do. We restore *order* with imagination. We instill *hope* again and again and again."
Thus, humans don't just think; we think (predominantly) in terms of story (narrative).

As advanced thought-creatures, we use these story-like thought mechanisms all day long, 24/7.

Think about it: Why would anyone tell a long story about their kid's horrific and uncomfortable first day at school when they can get straight to the point and say, "They felt like a fish out of water."

The term many cognitive linguists use for such language apparatus is "compression."[7] Another key word and concept we'll use throughout this work is scripting.

The term "scripting" fits well for a few reasons.

First, scripting is what screenwriters, producers, and directors do to ensure any story (play, movie, show) and its characters retain their integrity.

Second, scripting is programmatic; it's how computer programmers make a series of instructions (written programs) run automatically and instantaneously, so those instructions don't need to be programmed again.

Third, scripting underscores the very idea that we think metaphorically, using language devices to promote ideas and solve problems. Exhibit one: *"Everything is a F*cking Story."*

Humans learn from experience – our own and others' – and unconsciously script, writing and storing code for future reference. In short, we programmatically package thoughts into automated thought patterns (habits), similar in many ways to the "IF-THEN" scripts computer programmers use to save time and energy. [5]

An IF-THEN script looks something like this:
IF *ABC (is observed or happens; this might be considered a trigger or cue)*, THEN I will think/do *XYZ*.

Isn't this precisely what the Heider and Simmel research participants did? They were asked to observe a simple animation. However, nearly all of them referenced their own stored scripts. They inferred meaning and drew conclusions; they crafted a story, and it all happened instantly, *without awareness.*

It's almost as though each observer silently began handing out scripts: "OK, (Big Triangle) you – you're the father; you're the bully, and you're gonna act this way. And you (Circle), you're the worried mother, so you're gonna act this way. And you (Little Triangle), well, you're the angry teenager. Thus, you're gonna be the rebel!"[6]

Wait!!!

It (the 90-second clip) was simply a rudimentary animation of a couple of triangles and a circle moving in and out of a rectangle!

---

[5] In "The Stories That Freakin' Matter" chapter, I share examples of personal if-then scripts gone "sideways."
[6] In multiple presentations, a domestic violence "scene" was described.

Let's try this: There are three random items on a table: a beverage, a nail, and a sweater. Very random.

If you consider each long enough, a *narrative* is likely to emerge.

That sweater? Oh, it's beautiful! Just like the one Auntie used to wear, and boy, do I miss Auntie.

The nail? Huh, reminds me of the flat tire I got last week, and darn, it's frustrating when people let nails loose on the roads.

The diet soda? That sh*t is dangerous! The ingredients are so unhealthy. I gotta remember to throw away all our diet sodas!

And that's just with objects. It turns out that when there are characters – even potential characters, such as triangles and circles – our stories go into overdrive!

Granted, these aren't Shakespearean-type stories, but they are bite-sized narratives – programmed thought scripts – designed to complete, compress, round out, refine, and *accelerate* our thinking.

Legend has it that Ernest Hemingway, the American short story writer, journalist, and novelist, was asked to pen a story using just six words. He responded:

"For Sale: baby shoes, never worn."[8]

Potent! Some people tear up after reading that "story." Those six words aren't meaningful in and of themselves. Instead, they're powerful because of the story you immediately inferred. Did you notice how your mind raced to fill in the details?

Did you notice that *it* happened automatically?

Did you happen to *"jump to a conclusion?"*

Here's the good and bad news: We do this largely without awareness.

This point is worth repeating: Our thought process is enhanced, accelerated, and, dare I say, more complete when framed by story. Rarely are we aware of these automated thought mechanisms. It's rare for humans to think about how we think, a process that, for the most part, is habitual – on autopilot.

We don't just think "sweater," "nail," or "soda." We tend to bring baggage (or perhaps luggage) to each situation we observe.

Speaking of which, you do know the difference between baggage and luggage, right?

An old friend loves to share a *story* about my father, who is known for his sardonic wit.

As my parents were loading up their car after a quick visit to San Diego, I said something like, "Dad, I got it; let me help you with the baggage."

Jumping at the opportunity to be funny, he looked at us and countered, "That's not baggage, Mart; it's luggage. Luggage is something you want to be carrying." Then, winking and nodding his head, tilting it toward my mother, he continued, "Then, there's baggage."

Stories.

We bring luggage and baggage, in the form of stories, to the thousands of little scenarios that populate our lives.

It turns out that psychology has a wonderful term for all this baggage we're lugging around: "gunnysacking." It's a metaphor for storing up all the emotional hurts, resentments, and grievances we've acquired over a lifetime of relationships and trials.

The term "gunnysacking" is based on the idea that we're all lugging around a gunny sack (burlap bag) that holds our emotionally charged events (stories). You know, like how you're entitled to think your boss is a jerk and resent them because they didn't let you take last week off. Or, how hanging on to the story about your electricity and gas being shut off because your spouse forgot to pay the utility bill will come in handy later when your spouse nags you to fix the sink.

The wrong story, carried around too long, will likely derail anyone. In contrast, the "right" story may be the best ally you could have.[7] One of my best friends growing up lost his high school sweetheart to a Hollywood celebrity in the late '80s. The actor is worth hundreds of millions of dollars. Twenty-plus years later, I still recall my buddy telling that story.

What stories are rattling around in your gunny sack? How many are deleterious? Deleterious is a word that derives from Greek and means "noxious," "destroyer," or

---

[7] More on this in the "Why?" chapter.

even "mentally or morally hurtful." Notice the prefix "delete" as your first clue to quickly abandon any story you recognize as non-serving!

A powerful Zen tale reminds us to assess our payload – to take inventory – often. It's a tale of two monks whose oath was to never to touch a woman.

One day, the two monks came upon a river they intended to cross. They noticed a young lady asking for assistance attempting to do the same. Without a word, the older monk lifted her on his back and proceeded to carry her across the river. Once there, he gently set her down and continued his journey.

The younger monk witnessed the incident in total disbelief. Not a word was spoken as the monks continued their trek. As they approached their destination, unable to restrain himself any longer, the younger monk wailed, "Why would you carry her on your back? You know we're not permitted to touch women!"

The elder monk responded swiftly, "My friend, I set her down on the other side of the river a while ago; why is it that *you* are still carrying her?"

Even though we may be mature adults, well into our 30s, 40s, 50s, and beyond, we may still carry an exceptional amount of emotionally charged baggage.

For the small percentage fortunate enough to notice the load, the following questions may be helpful: Do I need to carry this story any longer? How is this story serving me? Is there any way I can turn this baggage into luggage so that it might serve me or others in the future?

Initially, this book was about the notion and study of "right thought." At one point, it was titled *The Mind Refined*. However, as the ideas around thinking and meta-cognition continued to germinate, it finally became crystal clear what a "mind refined" and "Thought 2.0" are: **better stories**.

You may wonder, "What is a *better* story?" or, "If I'm just telling these stories to myself, why do they need to be 'better'"?

This book aims to help you discover your stories, sometimes like a forensic scientist and sometimes like an archeologist. You'll be asked to dig deep. You'll uncover old stories and explore new stories. You'll shine a spotlight on each and ultimately determine if a story serves you well, if it needs some reworking, or if it should be completely discarded.

You'll begin by observing your stories from afar, listening to the voices – the narrators – in your head. You'll learn to discern the various motivations behind these voices.

The objective is to observe your stories as though you have stepped off the train of thought and are no longer a passenger. After all, it's easier to see where the train is headed when you're not riding in it. As the late, great Yankee catcher Yogi Berra said, "You can observe a lot by watching."

The purpose of this work is to:

- Help you become a more effective thinker.
- Help you notice how you think predominantly in the form of stories and scripts relative to the "big" areas in your life.
- Help you to notice the stories you tell yourself about yourself and the world in which you live.
- Help you edit, delete, or completely discard the baggage – any non-serving stories.
- Understand what makes a good story vs. a debilitating, self-defeating story.
- Help you craft empowering, supportive stories that make achieving your goals and ideals more possible and easier.
- Finally, I venture to introduce a new behavior model, the "3 Circles of Behavior Echo-System." While the name hardly rolls off the tongue, it's already proven to simplify and articulate human behavior from one moment to the next. Further, it illustrates the core, fundamental influencers relative to long-term personal transformation and goal achievement and how your stories are at the heart of each.

So, watching and observing your stories, you'll ask, "Where is this story taking me? Is it carrying me closer or further from my ideals and goals? Is it a supportive, empowering story, or is it full of excuses, blame, or even shame? Does this story harm or build up other people?

What other versions of this story are possible?"
That's an important one.

What other versions of this story are possible?

Since you are the one *constructing* the story, you should often ask what other versions of the story are *possible*.

After all, you are already writing your stories!
You are not a lion.

You can, and should, with intention, write the stories that will glorify you and the world in which you live.

HYPNOTIZED!

"Without illusion, there can
be no enlightenment."
~Buddha

As I sketched some notes on a Saturday morning, my youngest daughter, Eva (16 at the time), walked past me.

"Eva!" I clearly interrupted her train of thought as she reached for the fridge. "Do you know you are *hypnotized!?*"

Before I tell you her response, I want to share a little background – a couple of Eva stories. Eva has always been one of the wittiest people I've known. Her quick wit has become semi-legendary among friends and family. Once, while watching a video with one of my buddies in it, at the age of six, she blurted out, "Who's the random bald guy?!"

At the age of nine, we received a letter from her Junior Lifeguard counselor, who summarized his experience with her like this: "Eva is one of my all-stars. On Shores Day, after a very cold swim around the buoy, all the kids were complaining about how cold and tired they were. Eva threw on her full suit, stood right in front of me, and said, 'So, are we snorkeling with the sharks now?'"

He finished with, "Awesome Eva!"

One more Eva *story*. When she was about 6, a friend was visiting with his daughter. As we headed toward the beach, we drove past a series of stop signs. Surprisingly, I was pulled over by a police officer.

Cop: "Do you know why I pulled you over?"

Me: "No, sir." I thought it was probably because I rolled through the stop sign.

Cop: "You aren't wearing your seat belt!"

Eva: (from the back seat of the car, shouting): "He never wears his seat belt!"

My buddy, the girls, and even the officer started laughing out loud. In a split second, I go from angry at Eva to thinking maybe her levity might pay off with a simple warning.

No such luck. I still got a ticket!

That is Eva, though.

So, when I queried her with, "Do you know you are hypnotized!?" can you guess how she responded instantly?

"If I were, how would I know?"

Stunned, I nearly fell out of my chair. Suddenly, I had the affirmation I didn't even know I sought. I was elated!

Now it's *our* turn.

Me: Do you know you are hypnotized?

You: If I were, how would I know?

Translation: Of course, I am freakin' hypnotized! We all are!

Now that we can agree to this golden awareness – that we're ALL walking around hypnotized – the important question becomes, what stories are we hypnotized to believe?

Carl Jung, the legendary Swiss psychiatrist and psychoanalyst, underscores this idea, suggesting, "The most important question anyone can ask is: What myth am I living?"

The Buddha allegedly said, "Without illusion, there can be no enlightenment." To enlighten ourselves, we must carry less, not more. We must recognize and shed the illusions, the stories that weigh us down and hold us back.

To shed or remove anything makes us lighter. This is the beginning of enlightenment: letting go, carrying less.

Recall the term "Gunnysacking" from the previous chapter, and it's easy to see how removing your gunny sack and letting go of these emotionally charged stories is liberating. Letting go of the scars and damage they've caused, even when you are entitled and justified to continue to carry them because you've "earned" the right.

Are they weighing you down?

How are these stories facilitating your goals?

Consider all your grudges, resentments, entitlements, rationalizations, justifications, excuses, judgments, opinions, and expectations (of yourself and others), just for starters – all of them are stories.

Each adds to your daily payload.

Just how many stories are in your gunnysack?
Which can you release now?

For example, how often have you heard: "I can't believe they still carry around that grudge."

In essence, the "grudge" doesn't exist. Whatever happened is in the past. In the now, that grudge is simply additional payload – another story.

This doesn't mean we shouldn't learn from our past. We must learn and understand our personal his*tory*. We do that best by assessing our stories, identifying their lessons, and discarding the rest.

Thus, it's time to awaken now and pay excruciating attention to the countless stories you carry around about everything.

Introduction

PROLIFIC

> *"You're never going to kill storytelling because it's built into the human plan. We come with it."*
> ~Margaret Atwood

You are one of the most prolific storytellers in the universe.

By universe, I mean *your* universe. By prolific, I'm referring to the sheer quantity of stories you tell yourself. And, by stories, I mean all those little narratives, the ones you reiterate to yourself all day long.

You tell yourself stories about your career, finances, fitness, health, relationships, and countless daily experiences and observations – even about the goals you may or may not be trying to achieve.

Given the pervasiveness of the stories woven throughout your life, when was the last time you performed an analysis?

When was the last time you took inventory of all the stories you tell yourself about yourself, your family, your work and professional life, your well-being, and your health?

Unfortunately, for many, the answer is *never*.

No matter the topic, I'm reasonably sure you could rattle off a story. The beauty is, you don't have to be Shakespeare, Oprah, Lin-Manuel Miranda, Ronald Reagan, Churchill, or any of history's great storytellers, because the stories you tell are to an audience of ONE.

And, when it comes to your stories, you, my friend, are the judge, jury, and executioner!

There's the story about how great or horrible your job is, the story about your parents and your childhood, your pet, your boyfriend or girlfriend, your spouse, and even your third-grade teacher. There's a story about your health, fitness, injuries, or impairments, as well as the goals and aspirations you can or cannot reach.

You have forward-looking stories, stories about the present, and stories about your past. Each story influences, directs, and shapes your life.

As therapist Lori Gottlieb put it in her terrific TED Talk, "Change Your Stories, Change Your Life," "We assume that circumstances shape our stories. But what I've found time and again in my work is that *the exact opposite happens; the way we narrate our lives shapes what they become.*"

"The way we narrate our lives shapes what they become."

Now, hold Lori's statement up against James Allen's observation from the early 1900s, "You are today where your thoughts have brought you; you will be tomorrow where your thoughts take you." The implications are inescapable: Our "thoughts" direct our future.

By "thoughts," I mean *stories*.

Consider the breadth of your stories, and you'll notice something powerful: They tend to mirror and *affirm everything*, from your overall happiness to your wellness and peace of mind.

The reason for such affirmation is traced to a couple of unique and peculiar psychological traits: One, humans are self-justifying creatures, and two, we often, unconsciously, practice something referred to as confirmation bias. Psychologically speaking, that simply means we are wired to seek out information – evidence – that reinforces the narratives we tell ourselves and others.

An example of confirmation bias is finding evidence everywhere that supports whichever narrative you may be crafting, perhaps even selling, from "your spouse is a cheat" to "your boss is a jerk."

Thus, your most repeated stories – the ones you narrate over and over – habitually – gain the most traction, directing and steering your life.

Story after story, day after day, week after week. A lifetime of stories told silently to yourself, each tapping your attention, focus, and emotional resources. A cacophony of mental chatter, reminding me of the classic Zen parable.

The first monk observed, "The flag is moving."

The second monk countered, "No, it is the wind that is moving."

A Zen master, in passing, overhears and then silences their argument, "It is your mind that is moving."

Perpetual mental chatter, every day, all day long, story after story that may sound like:

Story: "Why did he say that to me as I was leaving for work? He is so ungrateful!"

ToS (The other Story): Is he really ungrateful? Was he ungrateful last week when he brought home flowers?

Story: "Why is she always spending money? We must be saving money now more than ever! She keeps this up, we'll be in the poor house."

ToS: Didn't she spend money on summer school for the kid, nothing frivolous? Was there an option?

Story: "I'd love to exercise, but I simply don't have any time to work out!"

ToS: Interesting. How many people have more than 24 hours a day?

Story: "Oh, they just want us to think they have their sh*t together. They're all so phony!"

ToS: Chances are, they aren't even thinking about you or the judgment you're projecting on them.

At this point, you may be thinking, "Those aren't stories; they're harmless little assumptions, thought vignettes, maybe even attitudes of mind."

Perhaps, but is it wrong to counter that any substantial attitude of mind is formulated, reinforced, and buttressed by story?

What happens when these "little assumptions" – these *scripts* – go unnoticed, unchecked, and are repeated for days, weeks, months, perhaps years?

Besides draining our limited energy, they direct our attention and focus.

Every story has a cost.

Each story has a price, and the price is paid every time you engage in *any* narrative.

What's the price?

Well, every time you tell yourself one story, you can't tell yourself another.

You can only tell yourself one story at a time.

Thus, every story has an opportunity cost.

While there may be dozens of stories running in the background, almost like an undercurrent or another computer program, just one story runs in the foreground; only one story has your attention and focus *now*.

Hopefully, *this* is it.

So, the cost is exceptionally high – arguably priceless – as you can never regain lost time.

Recall William James or even the Buddha's profound observation from the Preface – their most fundamental lesson: One becomes what one thinks about, most of the time. Or, consider William Blake's precious observation, "We become what we *behold*."

What stories are you beholding, most of the time?

If your thinking is predominantly in the form of story, driving various storylines within your life, it's essential to assess the narratives you tell most often.

As your time and attention are the primary conductors of your behavior, which are responsible for your productivity and achievement, the cost of misapplied or inaccurate storytelling or "beholding" is beyond measure.

It is this selective beholding of such narratives, from one moment to the next, which constitutes a *"mind refined."*[8]

As most of your stories are on repeat mode rather than going away, they do the opposite: grow in force and magnitude. So, these "harmless" little assumptions, "thought vignettes," or attitudes of mind, gain steam and gather momentum with every "play."

In some cases, these stories become so thoroughly developed that they even include heroes and villains.

Imagine that!

So, who are the villains and the heroes in your life?

The good news is it doesn't have to be *all* bad news.

The same superpower of story – Thought 2.0 – that drags us down and can pull us far off course can similarly guide our lives with intention and purpose. Yet, that can only happen with *awareness.*

---

[8] This was the title we almost settled on for this book!

With awareness, one grabs the helm – the steering wheel – and intentionally directs and cultivates the storylines that will serve them.

Thus, it's no exaggeration to suggest that one of your greatest superpowers is your capacity to craft, direct, edit, and curate the stories you tell yourself *daily*.

Once again, leaning on William James, the great philosopher, historian, and the first educator to offer a psychology course in the United States: "The greatest discovery of my generation is that human beings can alter their lives by altering their attitudes of mind."

By "attitudes of mind," James means our personal narratives.

And, if James' premise is correct, then the mandate is clear: **It's time to tell yourself better stories.**

Which begs the question, "How do you know if your stories are good or worthwhile?"

Here's the answer (drumroll, please):
Examine your life.

Examine your life's results.

Look around. Look in the mirror.

Chances are excellent that the results you're experiencing right now are a mirror-like reflection of the stories you've told yourself thus far.

Review your financial stories and compare them to the current state of your finances. How about your relationship status? Does your story match your results? What about your fitness story? Is there any coincidence there?

Undoubtedly, there are a handful of readers saying, "This is total bullsh*t! My stories are only projecting my circumstances – my current reality – not creating it!"

"My job sucks! My boss is a jerk, and my wife is constantly nagging me. She takes me and all my hard work for granted! I can tell you right now, this ain't no F'in story – this is my reality!"

Fair enough.

But ask yourself about causality. Do you believe in the law of cause and effect? ("From what does an oak tree grow?")

Once again, from therapist Lori Gottlieb's brilliant TED talk, "*Change your Story Change your Life*" (cited earlier):

"We assume that circumstances shape our stories. But what I've found time and again in my work is that the exact opposite happens; the way we narrate our lives shapes what they become."

Stephen Covey, the author of *The Seven Habits of Highly Effective People*, put it this way: "The only thing that endures over time is the 'Law of the Farm.' You must prepare the ground, plant the seed, cultivate, and water if you expect to reap the harvest."

What is "the planting of the seed"? That "seed" represents your stories.

Chances are good that long before your spouse was constantly nagging you, you two were harmonious. After all, you did get married, right?

There's a point in relationships when behaviors may begin to change, and perhaps the little kindnesses are lost.[9]

Remember, our thinking (narratives) drives our emotions, decisions, and actions. When it comes to relationships, there's a golden rule: Each person is 100% responsible.

There isn't just 100% to be divided among the two disgruntled parties. Each party owns 100% interest in the outcome and success of any relationship endeavor.

***

One of the most fascinating aspects of *story* is its definition:[10]

**sto· ry | \ ˈstȯr-ē **

    plural stories

    1a: an account of incidents or events

     b: a statement regarding the facts pertinent to a situation

    c: ANECDOTE

        especially: an amusing one

    2a: a fictional narrative shorter than a novel

            specifically: SHORT STORY

    b: the intrigue or plot of a narrative or dramatic work

    3: a widely circulated rumor

    4: LIE, FALSEHOOD

    5: LEGEND, ROMANCE

    6: *a news article or broadcast*

    7: MATTER, SITUATION

    8: Archaic

        a: HISTORY sense 1

Did you happen to notice it?

Do you see what makes the definition of story so peculiar?

By definition, story is both FACT and FICTION.

This is known as a Janus word, contronym, or auto-antonym. It's a word that is its own opposite. While we won't review this phenomenon in detail, it's worth remembering just how *nonsensical* this is.

And, it means that *EVERYTHING* is a f*cking story.

***

In the world of software development, there's a great acronym that fits perfectly here. At its core, it's all about responsibility: **GIGO** (Garbage In, Garbage Out).

The quality of the output – the results any computer program produces – is directly correlated to the quality of the input – the programming or scripting.

In life, there is no escaping this truth:

You are the programmer. Thus, you are responsible for the quality of the input (programming).

Your thoughts—*stories* are the input, and your results are the output.

Garbage In. Garbage Out.

Good In. Good Out. Greatness In. Greatness Out

As you are the programmer, it's your choice.

Now, it's important to distinguish results from circumstances. Many circumstances have environmental causes, such as earthquakes, hurricanes, pandemics, illness, death, a recession, and "acts of God" – the list is long. Such environmental influences occur separately from our input (programming) and control. Yet, within each circumstance and event, we retain control of our thoughts, attitudes, and stories.

Our environment often acts as a superior external force. Yet, we retain the ability to choose our **response**, and, worth noting, our response is guided and framed by the stories we tell ourselves.

Our response is guided and framed by the stories we tell ourselves.

My father, a former executive in the finance industry, used to share the popular axiom, "A rising tide lifts all boats." In a good economy, *all* stocks go up. In a recession, *all* stocks go down, and environment trumps story and strategy, at least in the near term.

The Covid-19 pandemic provides numerous examples of how environmental events impact lives. Consider the thousands of capable and thriving entrepreneurs whose businesses were shut down by governmentally directed initiatives designed to limit the spread of the virus.

Yet, despite examples like this, there are still many self-help gurus who claim that one's thinking is 100% responsible for all the circumstances in their life. They say things like, "There are no accidents."

Unfortunately, such claims are silly, dichotomous, careless, confusing, and ultimately hurtful to those whose lives are impacted by horrific external events.

The unavoidable fact is that accidents, tragedies, and generally sh*tty hands are dealt to people all the time. In fact, an entire industry – the insurance industry – exists solely because accidents happen – often.

There are many things within our control *and* many things outside of our control.

Simply put: It's your job to know the difference.

Thus, an essential principle – perhaps the very first precept of "better," "right," or "effective" thinking – is being able to discern which results we're responsible for and which are beyond our influence and control.

Understanding what we do control and influence and what we do not is just the first pillar of "better thinking." Within Buddhism, this is identified as "Right View," and not coincidentally, it is the very first path in what they call "The Noble Eightfold Path."

"Right View" is understanding events and circumstances as they are, assuming responsibility where it is necessary, and understanding that our actions have consequences.

The better we can identify and manage our stories with awareness, responsibility, and precision, the better they can serve us, directing and influencing our behaviors, decisions, and actions – our habits.

In order to do this, it's essential to first examine the code – our STORIES.

THREE CIRCLES (THE REDUX)

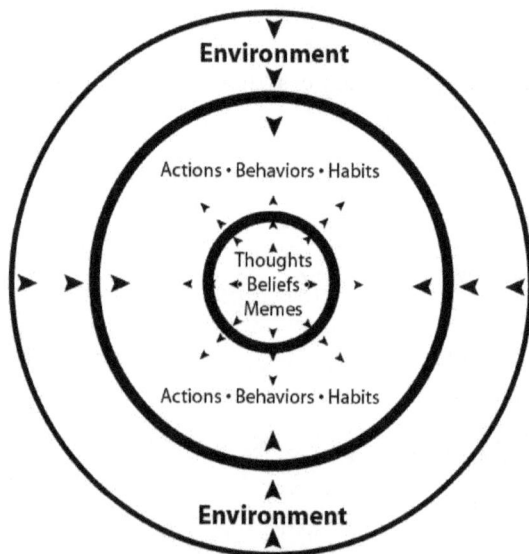

Environment

Actions • Behaviors • Habits

Thoughts
Beliefs
Memes

Actions • Behaviors • Habits

Environment

(Originally the "3 Circles Model," published in *The Pressure Paradox*, 2015)

"Everything must be made as simple as possible.
But not simpler."[9]
~ Albert Einstein

The following is an excerpt from the 2015 edition of *The Pressure Paradox*. Its purpose is to illustrate the parameters of human behavior and psychology in their most simplistic form.

---

[9] Reportedly a condensed interpretation/translation from a 1933 lecture.

***

Analyze the diagram above carefully. In simple terms, it represents the entire context of human behavior, bookended and influenced by two worlds: our inner, invisible world (thoughts) and our outer, physical world (environment).

Since the dawn of man, the great philosophers have promoted and taught that it is the "first world," our thoughts (the inner world), that directly influences and impacts our outer world. In fact, in the late 1800s, William James proclaimed, "The greatest revolution of our generation is the discovery that human beings, by changing the inner attitudes of their minds, can change the outer aspects of their lives."

[End of excerpt from *The Pressure Paradox*]
***

What was once "The Three Circles" has evolved into the "3 Circles of Behavior Echo-System." It's both a model and a framework. It is a visual representation of how energy and information flow and influence each major component within a perpetual behavior echo-system.

Here's the updated behavior model:

Updated:
The 3 Circles of Behavior Echo-System

© equilibrium enterprises, inc.
2017 - 2022

everythingastory.com

The following elements have evolved:

1. **Story**: This book's thesis emphasizes the inner circle – the powerful idea that *story* is the primary means of cognitive function and analysis, conducting our decisions, actions, and behaviors, influencing habits and skills, and forging achievements and results. No prevalent behavior-change model represents the human thought process as story.[11]

2. **Emotions and feelings**: After further meditation and collaboration, the borders within the concentric circles must include a passageway – conduits between each influencing layer or component circle. Thus, emotions and feelings must be recognized as conduits within the echo-system.[10]

3. **Bidirectionality**: The arrows between the major influencers have evolved to become bidirectional. This better illustrates how each primary component circle (environment, behaviors, thoughts) "echoes" back and forth, altering our emotions and feelings and influencing the other layers.

4. **Non-linear/non-circular representation**: Two of the most prevalent behavior change models, Cognitive Behavior Therapy (CBT), considered the gold standard, and Transtheoretical Model (TTM), represent human behavior in a circular fashion.[11] The echo-system provides a new representation of how energy and information flow and how they reverberate relative to our behaviors and thoughts depending on their forcefulness. Further, an echo-system underscores timeless principles like cause and effect and even karma.

---

[10] We cover feelings and emotions in greater detail in the "How?" chapter.
[11] Behavior model images shown in the coming pages.

5. **Awareness**: The 3 Circles of Behavior Echo-System articulates how, with awareness, we can proactively alter our behavior by changing our thoughts (stories) and/or environment.

6. **The Environment**: The all-encompassing environment is both the sensory **input** and the **output** – our results. The environment is something we can change, and it's something that influences our thoughts, feelings, emotions, and behaviors.

7. **Simplicity**: Finally, the 3 Circles of Behavior Echo-System, by comparison, is a straightforward model. It follows Einstein's basic commandment: "Everything must be made as simple as possible, but not simpler." Simplicity tends to equate to practicality and use, increasing effectiveness.

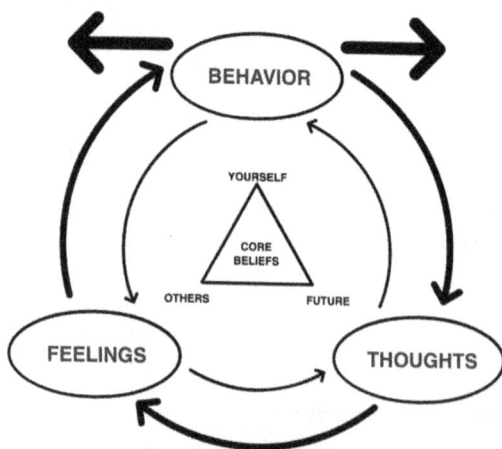

Cognitive Behavior Therapy (CBT)

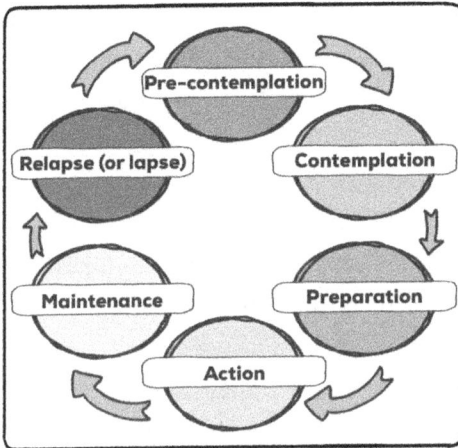

Transtheoretical Model (TTM)

The 3 Circles of Behavior Echo-System

© equilibrium enterprises, inc.
2017 - 2022

everythingastory.com

This behavior echo-system provides anyone with the clichéd 30,000-foot overview to better guide them from being a reactionary participant to someone in a position of *response-ability*.

This model illustrates how, over the long haul, *environment* and *story* are the most significant influencers of our behaviors, habits, and skills.

Important: The interaction among the three major influencers in this echo-system – stories, habits/behaviors, and environment – is not always linear. For example, an environmental change might impact your story seemingly before affecting your behavior or emotions. Nonetheless, all components influence and affect each other perpetually.

Example:
A person steps on a subway train at night in an unsafe part of the city. The change in environment and their situational awareness spark the narrative that their safety may be threatened. This is an example of environment directly affecting someone's story first. What action does the person take? They clutch their bag tightly. Environment – (influences) -> Story –(influences) -> Action/Behavior.

With the above model (and the three books taken as a whole), *The Habit Factor*, *The Pressure Paradox*, and now, *Everything*, the intention is to provide a simplified model and framework for lasting, positive change and personal transformation.

This simply means that for any goal or ideal, relative to personal transformation, the 3 Circles of Behavior Echo-System acts as a simplified checklist – a cheat sheet – for goal achievement and positive behavior change.

Important: All lasting behavior change requires these three major components to be congruent:

STORY (inner circle)
HABITS/SKILLS (middle circle)
ENVIRONMENT (outer circle)

While skills/behaviors and thinking/mindset are self-explanatory, when it comes to the environment, there may be some confusion. We'll take a moment to examine the concept of environment.

Environment defined: In the 3 Circles of Behavior Echo-System, the environment represents both sensory **input** (stimulus) and the **output** – outcomes and results.

Inputs are cues and triggers, including circumstances, events, and the physical environment – everything that provides sensory input to affect your feelings, emotions, thinking, and behaviors. Examples include family, friends, physical surroundings, and random events (accidents, chance). Even your body provides environmental input. If something is outside of your thinking, emotions, and behaviors, it's part of your environment.

Importantly, the environment also includes your outputs. Your outputs are your results – what you affect and produce.

Your outputs may be the consequences of your actions, decisions, behaviors, habits, and skills. As we mentioned above, your body is part of your environment. For example, a bodybuilder experiences results that reveal their skills, habits, and behaviors. Their body (environment) is transformed.

Everything we produce and affect in our environment becomes a stimulus (sensory input). Thus, a perpetual behavior-change echo-system is in effect.

Here are some examples of the behavior-change echo-system in action:

1. **Outside→in behavior change:**
   A comet strikes just outside your house! (Environment).
   You feel the Earth shake. You're instantly startled and scared! (Feelings/Emotions)
   You run out of your house. (Behaviors/Actions)
   You begin to think, "The world is ending!" (Thoughts/Story)

   Summary: The environment directs and influences your feelings and emotions, directly influencing your actions and behaviors, which direct and influence your thoughts and story.

2. **Inside→out behavior change:**
   You wake up one morning with the narrative that
   the world and life are hopeless. "It's all ending soon
   anyway." (Thought/Story)
   These thoughts (your story) influence your feelings.
   You feel sad and hopeless. (Feelings/Emotions)
   You call a friend later that morning.
   (Behaviors/Actions)
   Your friend comes over to talk with you and
   comfort you. (Environment change.)

Summary: Your thoughts and story direct and influence
your feelings and emotions, which direct and influence your
actions and behaviors, which cause an environment change.

**You may be thinking, "So what? Why should I care
about any of this?"**
Here's why: Despite having a supportive environment
and possessing the requisite skills and habits, my stories
were *misaligned*. This simple behavior model could've saved
me years of confusion. What's the value of that?
Further, since change is one of the great constants in
life, setting goals allows us to guide and direct the changes
we'd like to see (most of the time). This behavior model
reveals the path to do so.
Arguably, many never attempt to achieve their most
important goals or aim toward their full potential because
there is no clear model, map, or process showing the way.

This behavior model and book reveal the path.

A bold statement. But understanding the fundamental components of behavior change, personal transformation, and goal achievement – how this Behavior Change Echo-System works – allows anyone to determine where (in which component influencer) to *begin* their journey.

Would you like to start by modifying your thinking? A new narrative can undoubtedly help you drive new emotions that will foster new actions – the beginning of new habits and skills. (Personal example below.) We'll get more into the nuts and bolts of new narratives in the chapter called "The Stories That Really Freakin' Matter.")

Do you want to begin your journey of personal transformation by changing your environment? This could be as simple as rearranging your office or furniture, altering your refrigerator or pantry inventory, joining a support group, or finding a different peer group to associate with.

Or, you can begin with my personal favorite, intentionally tracking your behaviors to help form the new, positive habits that will ultimately change your narratives, stories, habits, and environment.

Lasting transformation is metamorphosis. By definition, metamorphosis often demands new habits (and skills). Therefore, any time you desire, you can initiate transformation by beginning with *any* of the three component influencers:

(1) Thoughts/Stories ☐
(2) Behavior/Skills/Habits ☐
(3) Environment ☐

What I find curious is that individuals not only have learning preferences and biases but also have preferences for initiating their own behavior change. Most of the time, they aren't aware of it.

When I teach the 3 Circles Behavior Echo-System, I'll ask participants to reflect upon a recent behavior change effort, either successful or unsuccessful. A student who appeared excited by this model shared: "This is interesting! I tend to start with my environment. I bought a book recently." Then, they laughed, "It's sat on my bookshelf ever since."

Some people prefer to initiate behavior change with their environment – a class, coach, course, teacher, support group, or even a book. Others tend to put the spotlight on the related personal narrative (their "Why?" story)[12], as in *why* they must change their behavior and develop new habits. They know that a new story will drive compelling feelings and emotions followed by actions.

Finally, this critical message about transformation and personal metamorphosis bears repeating:

Each major component (circle) must be engaged and congruent for lasting transformation.

Ultimately, your story, skills/habits, and environment must all be involved and aligned to foster legitimate, lasting change.

---

[12] See the "Why?" chapter.

We'll look at a few basic examples of the Behavior Change Echo-System in action:

***

Let's begin with a classic comedy movie to which many people (at least in the U.S.) can probably relate: *Trading Places*, starring Eddie Murphy.

The movie (story) brilliantly illustrates how environment influences our behaviors and results. This is an example of Outside→In behavior change).

In the film, directed by John Landis and starring Dan Aykroyd and Eddie Murphy, two wealthy men, Randolph and Mortimer Duke, who run a commodities brokerage firm, decide to make a wager. They want to see if changing someone's circumstances will change their behaviors, habits, and skills – their character.

They hope this "little experiment" will help to settle an ongoing debate: nature (character) vs. nurture (environment). The question is: Will someone's character (actions and behaviors) be dramatically influenced by their immediate environment – how they're nurtured?

To do this, they replace one of their most successful investment managers, Winthorpe (Dan Aykroyd), with a random guy living on the street, Valentine (Eddie Murphy).

The story, said to have been inspired by Mark Twain's, *The Prince and The Pauper*, demonstrates how someone's environment (socioeconomic environment, in this case) directs their thoughts, actions, and behaviors.

Winthorpe, once a hard-working, upper-class commodities broker, quickly becomes a thief who uses drugs; he's despondent and suicidal. Meanwhile, Valentine, who was living on the street, is transformed into a happy, honest, hard-working, and wealthy commodities broker.

To summarize: The wealthy guy turns into a thief/beggar with loose morals, and the thief/beggar turns into a wealthy guy with a noble character.

The story illustrates how someone's environment (the outer circle) can dramatically alter their behaviors, decisions, actions/habits (Middle Circle), and thoughts/stories (Inner Circle).

The story's "little experiment" drives Winthorpe to the edge; hopeless (carrying a narrative about a hopeless future), he attempts suicide. Interestingly, he's saved by a woman (Jamie Lee Curtis) fostering a narrative of a hopeful future.

Spoiler alert: Mortimer Duke loses the bet and pays Randolph $1.

***

Another example, much closer to home, is my personal story. It's the creation story responsible for The Habit Factor (book and app), and it's a potent example of *Inside* → *Out* behavior change.

Shortly after my 35th birthday, driven by a mild case of depression combined with a great sense of frustration, I was desperate, searching; I felt stuck. I wanted to experience something new, different – some real progress in my life. The next thing I knew, I found myself engaged in a bucket list-type exercise.

I didn't have the awareness in the moment, but looking back, it was clear I just needed a spark – a catalyst – something to shake me out of my normalized day-to-day routine and eliminate the feeling of being trapped and overwhelmed by comfort.[13]

Side note: Perhaps not mentioned enough in behavior science is the profound relationship between the absence of pressure and depression. Healthy life challenges create pressure and growth, fostering strength and the feeling of being alive. Trees need wind; they require resistance – something to strengthen their roots. (This analogy and phenomena hold true even meteorologically speaking: When atmospheric pressure drops, a "depression" ensues – a literal loss of pressure. Rarely does nature say one thing and wisdom another.)[12]

Back to my Habit Factor story: At the time, it seemed I needed a new direction – a different destination. I felt like I was leaving a fair amount of my life – the life I wanted to experience – on the table. I felt as if I wasn't tapping into my full potential.

Out of desperation, I engaged in a Tony Robbins thought experiment that he termed "The Rocking Chair." The directive was to imagine myself at 85 and reflect happily upon all my amazing life experiences and achievements.

---

[13] Throughout this book, the term "desire" is used as a requisite for skill and habit development as well as goal achievement. Some identify this as motivation or leverage. *Desire* provides the initial force – pressure – to ignite change and fuel for the ongoing pursuit despite setbacks.

As I began to do this, the thought experiment evolved, and I accelerated the timetable. Rather than being 85, I convinced myself that I would die tomorrow!

I convinced myself that my life was over; my time was up. It was game over.

I fully subscribed to the *story* of my immediate demise.

It was completely made up, and I believed it.

It was visceral; I welled up with regret.

What have I done with my life?
What have I not done!?
What have I not achieved?
What have I not experienced?
How much time have I wasted?

Big, important questions I'd never bothered to ask or answer, all of which forced a sense of urgency – pressure – that would provide the combustion I needed to act!

The truth was, other than perhaps a bit of depression and disappointment with myself, I was in fine health.

However, emotionally charged with a story of my demise and the realization that my time had expired, I began scratching out a list – a bucket list – of experiences and achievements I deeply hoped to have before I died. [13]

At the very top of the list was a strange revelation: an event known as The Catalina Classic, a 32-mile open-ocean paddleboard race. This was an event I had talked about doing since I was 18 years old. "Someday, I'll do it!" Suddenly, it was 17 years later, and that "someday" never came.

I was so worked up emotionally by my death story that I threatened myself. "It's now or never! **Forget about the Catalina Classic forever or commit now!"**

Next thing I knew, I was running down my stairs. I jumped on the computer and began searching, hopeful I might find a website that would allow me to sign up for the event.

Inside→Out behavior change/transformation.

My story was so intense it provided a visceral reaction:

Story led to emotion, which led to action.
(Inner Circle) Story→ *Emotion*[14]
("membrane"/conduit)→ *Action*! (Middle Circle)→Environment!

The 3 Circles of Behavior Echo-System in full effect.

That imagination exercise – a deliberately crafted story – was the catalyst that led to completing one of the most meaningful goals in my life. More importantly, it redirected my life.

The real gem, though, was the unexpected gift: an innovative process that anyone could follow for effective and efficient habit development specifically designed to facilitate goal achievement. This process focused on crafting

---

[14] If you're wondering why emotions and feelings aren't more emphasized in the three-circle framework, we address this in the final Q&A section.

and aligning core, related behaviors (habits) instead of a series of "next steps" or an endless to-do list.

This process ultimately became known as The Habit Factor method, something I've been fortunate enough to teach worldwide to scores of individuals, companies, and organizations.

All of it, arguably, sparked by a "dumb little story" – a simple imagination exercise.

Parenthetically, one might argue, as others have, that my transformation journey didn't begin with my "demise" story; instead, it was triggered by feelings of depression and "stuck-ness."

Such an observation perfectly reinforces the prior statement: The 3 Circles of Behavior Echo-System is perpetually echoing back and forth, influencing each component.

Thus, much like any story, there is an arbitrary starting and ending.[15]

Another example of Outside→In transformation.

Jimmy, 48, is approximately 45 pounds overweight. Jimmy enrolls in a weight-loss program. The weight-loss program provides a support group and counselor. These elements alter his environment.

---

[15] For the rest of the story, check out *The Habit Factor*.

EVERYTHING Is A F*cking Story

Additionally, the new environment provides him with tools he can use to track his behaviors. They give Jimmy a workbook and direct him to use The Habit Factor habit tracker. These environmental influences (support group, counselor, workbook, and The Habit Factor habit tracker) aid him in fostering the belief that he will improve his habits for good.

Thus, Jimmy's narrative (belief) and self-concept[16] begin to change! Over time, the combined influence of his altered environment, his behavior (habit tracking), and his new story are aligned! After just three months, Jimmy's already lost 27 pounds.

Jimmy fully subscribed to the process his counselor at the weight loss center (Outer Circle) advised. He loves his new habits (Middle Circle), and, even more importantly, he subscribes to his new story (Inner Circle).

Jimmy doesn't worry about his weight rebounding because his **story**, **habits**, and **environment** are all congruent.

A final Outside→In behavior-change example:

The Covid-19 pandemic forced, by way of law, environmental changes to people's behavior. Everyone (most people) began to wear masks and social distance. Over time, the combination of environmental and behavioral changes influenced our thinking.

---

[16] More on the self-concept in the next section.

This is where the story gets interesting (pun intended). Over time, people's narratives evolved, in some cases, in radically different directions. To some, the pandemic was a hoax; to others, it was a life-and-death struggle.

Those whose stories remained aligned with the governmental laws (environment) implemented the behavior changes and continued to wear masks and social distance. Those whose narratives deviated from the government mandates ignored the laws and quickly restored old behaviors and habits.

This is a wonderful example of misalignment among the three concentric circles. The narrative of the "non-believers" didn't support the government-mandated behavior change.

Another key idea to be aware of is that when the environment is at odds with someone's story, their behavior (decisions, habits) will *primarily* align with their story.

In other words, when your environment and story compete head-to-head for your decisions, actions, and behaviors, your story tends to win.

However, this isn't always the case. For example, if you were threatened to be thrown in jail for not wearing a mask, you'd be far more likely to obey the government (environment), despite your competing story.

Therefore, when the environment is undeniable and overbearing, it wins, at least in the near term.

For example, say an earthquake disrupts your business and its infrastructure (plumbing, internet, electricity), as well as other local businesses. In this case, no matter how crafty, gritty, or empowering the story you hold about your company's resilience, you'd be unable to retain the same operational capacity, at least in the near term.

Not too long ago, a "thought leader" and author, who will remain anonymous, tweeted something along the lines of "systems and strategies will always trump your environment."

My response: "Apparently, you've never been in an earthquake."

When overbearing, the environment trumps personal narratives and forces new behaviors, systems, or strategies to adapt and evolve, at least in the near term.

This is why, for instance, Darwin's brilliant observation holds as true in business as it does in the natural world:

"It's not the strongest, nor the smartest of the species that survives, but the one that's most adaptable to change." [Read: Adaptable to the environment.]

***

Checklist: How to put the 3 Circles of Behavior Echo-System to work for you, particularly if you've struggled with behavior change.

Review these three essential components when it comes to your personal quest for transformation, particularly if efforts have fallen short.

1. **Your Story (Inner Circle)**: Assess and review the associated narrative and the scripts in your head relative to your desired goal.
    Be sure to review the *emotions* elicited by your story. Are the emotions substantial enough to inspire and ignite action?
    Yes: ☐   No: ☐

2. **Your Behavior/Habits (Middle Circle)**:
    To stay on track toward any goal, be sure to track the key related behaviors and habits:
a. To ensure new behavior and habit development efforts stay on track, it's extremely beneficial to track the intended new habits by following P.A.R.R.[14] [Plan, Act, Record, and Reassess]
    Are you tracking the key, related behaviors/habits that will lead you toward your goal's attainment?
    Yes: ☐   No: ☐

3. **Your Environment (Outer Circle)**:
    Is the environment supportive of your quest for personal transformation? Is your environment aligned

with and supportive of your goals and ideals, or is it at odds? (Remember, "environment" includes your friends, home, office, peer group, etc.)

For example, if your goal is to lose 15 pounds, and you still have potato chips in the pantry and ice cream in the freezer, the environment isn't conducive.
Is the environment supportive and conducive to the new habits you're trying to develop and the goals you're attempting to achieve?
Yes: ☐   No: ☐

By assessing the 3 Circles of Behavior Echo-System relative to your personal quest for transformation and goal achievement, you can intentionally design each to be aligned, supportive, and harmonious with your goals and ideals.[17]

---

[17] The "How?" chapter and Application exercises provide additional detail.

YOU'RE SOAKING IN IT!

"Storytelling is the most powerful way to put
ideas into the world."
~ Robert McKee, Professor

From the late 1960s through the '80s, Palmolive®
dishwashing soap ran a series of pervasive ads. The
commercials featured actress Jan Miner, the face of
Palmolive®, who portrayed "Madge."

Madge saved one woman after another from red,
chapped, dry, dishwashing hands by convincing them to
soak their hands in Palmolive®. She'd then surprise each
with the punchline, "You know, you're soaking in it!"

Stunned, each woman would respond incredulously,
"I'm soaking in it!? Dishwashing liquid!?" "Yep," Madge
assured each, "Palmolive® is more than mild, it gives me
suds that never stop, and it *softens hands while you do the dishes!*"
As if she knew of a great, universal secret that would change
the lives of homemakers forever.

Now, imagine for a minute that I'm Madge, and you are
my dishwashing friend.

Me: "You know you're soaking in it?"
You: "I am? Soaking in it? In what!?"
Me: "Stories!"

In 2005, David Foster Wallace began a brilliant commencement speech at Kenyon College with a short story. The tale goes something like this:

"There are these two young fish swimming along, and they happen to meet an older fish swimming the other way, who nods at them and says, 'Morning, boys. How's the water?'

"The two young fish continue swimming for a bit, then one of them asks the other, 'Water!? What the hell is water?'"

Whether it's water or dishwashing soap, I can assure you of one thing: You are swimming, soaking, perhaps even drowning in "it."

Stories.

Do me a favor, please.

Quickly and without much deliberation, rate your health and fitness level on a scale of 1 to 10 (with 10 being best).

I'm guessing there's a story behind that number.

Let's keep going, shall we? How about your:

Closest relationship.
Happiness level.
Professional career.

Please tell me how great or, depending on your disposition and attention, how f*cked up the world is right now.

There is little doubt that each of these stories (shared to yourself about your "situation") influences how you feel right now and will influence your life moving forward.

Story saturates everything.

Religion, arguably the foundation of civilization, is rooted in (drum roll, please) *story*.

Growing up, I was entirely captivated by Greek and Roman mythologies. I loved the stories of Hercules, Zeus, Pandora, and Athena. When our mother brought home Abyssinian kittens, I think seven in all, each was named after a Roman or Greek God (Athena, Pandora, Hercules, Zeus, Jupiter, Mars, Apollo).

Even my first dog (a miniature black Labrador) – a legend in his own right – taught me more about life and responsibility between the ages of 20 and 34 than any person or class I ever took. His name was Hercules.

It's an accepted fact that history is written by the victors who, at the expense of the enemy, glorify their cause. Napoleon famously observed, "What is history but a fable agreed upon?"

So, whether it's history (his-*story*), the daily news, Aesop's fables, music, religion, mythology, the latest Hollywood blockbuster, social media (Facebook and Instagram "Stories"), your favorite bestseller, or my current favorite, Zen koans, story is ubiquitous and permeates seemingly everything – the way we learn, think, observe, and even associate "things."

Psychology provides a fundamentally important concept known as "Locus of Control," posited by Julian B. Rotter in 1954, as a core influencer – a component of social learning theory. "Locus" derives from the Greek meaning "point" or location.

As you look out into the world, you process everything you observe and think uniquely. Thus, memoirist Anaïs Nin's powerful observation: "We don't see things as they are, we see them as we are."

The significance of that idea cannot be overstated.

At the epicenter – the heart – of each person's human experience is their unique psyche – defined as the "human soul, mind, or spirit." Each psyche has just one crucial job – a job no one else can do:

Steer their vessel – direct their life.

To steer any vessel, to captain any ship, we must assume responsibility. When it comes to your mind, responsibility begins with:

Keeping your hands on the steering wheel most of the time.

Your psyche is guiding your vessel right now. For better or worse, your psyche has delivered you to your current location.

Rather than gasoline, diesel, or wind, your vessel is guided by an exhaustible reserve: your energy and attention.

Where is your attention, most of the time?
Are your hands on the steering wheel?

Your attention at any moment is the collective association of your time and energy meeting at a particular point. Now, recall the Greek meaning of "locus" as "place," "spot," or "point," and you'll see how your attention is responsible for guiding your life.

If you have a pencil nearby, grab it. Hold the pencil in front of your face. Focus on its point. Then, keep your eyes on the tip of the pencil while you move it around. Notice how that awareness guides your thoughts.

That is the power of attention: What holds your attention tends to hold your future.[18]

everythingastory.com

---

[18] For those without sight, awareness is guided by other senses – touch, sound, feeling, etc. This is how inputs affect thoughts – story.

Further, story may serve as an evolutionary mechanism designed to prolong human attention. While other creatures might have attention spans that extend minutes, humans, backed by the capacity of story, can concentrate their attention upon ideas or problems for months or even decades.

What other creature can dwell on ideas for so long?

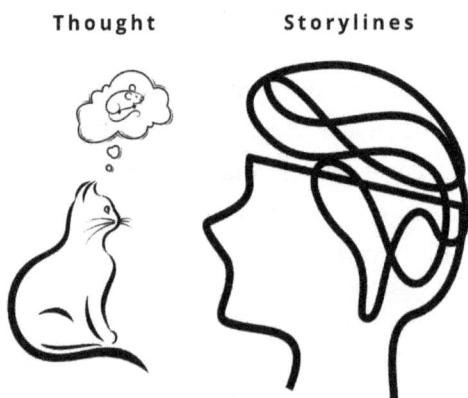

Thought   Storylines

everythingastory.com

Repeated, consistent attention toward a single idea, problem, cause, goal, or ambition is the only way anyone can steer themselves toward a desirable destination.

Concentration: Prolonged, focused attention upon a single idea or problem over an extended period is one of the most powerful achievement weapons. In fact, genius is often defined by that capability.

When it comes to your goals and ideals, how well formed are your stories? Do they excite you? Do they hold your attention? Are they doubtful or supportive of your ambitions? How often do you analyze, revisit, groom, and edit these stories?

Consider Buddha's alleged observation from the Preface: "Our life is shaped by our mind; we become what we think."

Does that mean that if I dwell upon a toaster, I will become a toaster? It's unlikely that any sane person believes they will become a toaster by thinking about a toaster.

It's also safe to assume that Buddha wasn't an idiot. Therefore, there must be a larger, implied context, and this is almost certainly it:

While you aren't likely to think about a toaster for too long, you will spend a lifetime dwelling upon Who and What you are and may become. Those are the stories that will establish your future's parameters and potential.

Thus, we *do* become what we think about, and those are the stories that steer our future.

Finally, it's important to point out that the Locus of Control theory was posited primarily to identify whether people believed they had influence over their future or were at the whim of the universe – external forces.

The short answer, as covered previously, is both – just as the definition of story is both factual and fictional. We are in control, and we are not in control – a crucial understanding.

We can direct and control our stories, most of the time. We can direct and control our behaviors, most of the time. We can control and direct our emotions, most of the time. We can control and affect our environment, **some** of the time.

The very act of choosing one storyline over another is an act of control.

Human control exists within a larger context of non-control. I have no control over whether a comet will strike the Earth or whether it's going to rain tomorrow.

I reiterate this crucial topic of control because many Goo-Roos insist, "Nothing is in our control." That's the sort of advice that is meant to help, yet it's debilitating and self-defeating.

Your stories – your imaginative narratives – are well within your control. Directing your prolonged concentration on the stories that really freakin' matter is your responsibility.[19]

Your stories saturate *everything*, from the most mundane daily experiences, such as why you elected to park your car in one spot over another, to life's most profound, existential, and philosophical questions, such as, "Why do humans exist? and "What's the meaning of life?"

All of it, story.

---

[19] More in the upcoming section, "The Stories that Really Freakin' Matter."

A Few Stories

*"If you ever find yourself in the
wrong story, leave."*
~ Mo Willems

*"There is an expiration date on blaming
your parents for steering you in the wrong
direction; the moment you are old enough to
take the wheel, responsibility lies with you."*
~ J.K. Rowling

MEANING

"Life has no meaning. Each of us has meaning,
and we bring it to life. It is a waste to be asking
the question when you are the answer."
~ *Joseph Campbell*

Famed author Joseph Campbell (1867-1954) was both a student and master of story. He was a professor of comparative literature and mythology for 38 years.

In the above passage, Campbell explains that because we are the writers, producers, and directors of our lives, our life's meaning is derived from the stories we've created or subscribed to.

"It's your life!" Campbell insists. "You're holding both the pen and paper!" Although, a pencil is an even better tool, as there are likely to be many edits along the way.

In Campbell's seminal work, *The Hero with a Thousand Faces* (1949), he proposed the theory of the Monomyth: the idea that, throughout history, the world's great mythologies all shared an archetypal format with something he termed "The Hero's Journey."

Within the Monomyth, Campbell asserts that the same core story – at its trunk – branches into dozens if not hundreds of variations. The Hero's Journey varies, but the essence remains the same. It's composed of three main parts:[15]

ACT 1: Departure
ACT II: Initiation
ACT III: Return

There's no shortage of great movie directors, writers, and producers who've subscribed to Campbell's storytelling formula, from George Lucas to Steven Spielberg, leveraging the Hero's Journey idea into cult sensations.

At the National Arts Club in 1985, *Star Wars* creator George Lucas commented on Campbell and his work: "This is it! After reading more of Joe's books, I began to understand how I could do this...Here's a lifetime of scholarship...It's possible that if I had not run across him [Campbell], I would still be writing *Star Wars* today."[16]

While the Hero's Journey may have as many as 17 different elements, one of the key ideas, for our purposes, is that the hero moves from a place of comfort, what we'll call the "**known world**," to a place of discomfort – in many cases *extreme* discomfort – and into the "**unknown world**."

The hero's "departure" happens by choice or chance; sometimes, a cosmic event beyond the hero's control thrusts them into the "unknown world."

It's worth pointing out that the force that *always* precipitates the hero's transformation is *pressure*.

Pressure, often extreme pressure, plays an essential role in the hero's transformation as they attempt to navigate a new and unknown world filled with challenges, obstacles, and uncertainty, producing feelings of profound discomfort, doubt, and fear.

Consider Dorothy in the *Wizard of Oz* and the tornado that swept her and Toto away. Or Alice in Wonderland deciding to follow the rabbit down the rabbit hole. Think about Luke Skywalker, who returns home to see his aunt and uncle's farm burned down by Imperial Stormtroopers.

These cataclysmic events thrust Dorothy, Alice, and Luke into adventure and the "unknown world."

The Hero's Journey, Wikipedia[17]

Before we go any further, it's crucial to point out the obvious: The Hero's Journey is far more about **YOU** and far less about Dorothy, Alice, or Luke Skywalker.

To recap:

A) It's *your* life.

B) It's *your* story.

C) Yes! **YOU** are the HERO.

Joe Rogan, host of the Joe Rogan Podcast Experience on Spotify, said it like this (love or hate him, the ideas are important):

> "What I tell people – the best advice I've ever heard [relative to personal development] is to live your life like you're the hero in your own movie, and *right now* is when the [f*ing] movie starts.
>
> Your life is a sh*tbag disaster (like every [f*ing] Arnold Schwarzenegger movie when he wakes up with a blender full of pizza and ice cream)…those guys are on the brink…they put the gun in their mouth, and they put it down because they see a picture of their daughter.
>
> Pretend that is you.
>
> Pretend you are in the part of the movie that starts and shows you as a [f*ing] loser. And just decide not to be a loser anymore.

Then, my favorite part:

> **"Live your life like there's a documentary crew following you around, and you're analyzing your own behavior.** Do what you'd want to do so that your kids would one day look back and see that documentary and look on it with pride like, "Wow, my dad was a bad [motherf*cker]. He really did what he had to do. Wow, my mom really got her [stuff] together."[18]

Acknowledging that you are the hero of your own story tends to elicit one of two responses, both rooted in fear.

The first response is deflection: "This is egotistical garbage! Why should I be the hero?! There are so many other people!"

The second, more common response is denial.

The fear arises once you realize it's your life, your story, and thus, you must be the hero. That's not to say you won't play other roles, such as mentor, guardian, student, sidekick, etc., but when it comes to *your* life, it's your movie. Thus, you must be the HERO.

Nobody can do your pushups for you.

Batman isn't doing Robin's pushups, either.

Imagine Superman taking to social media: "Why is everyone yelling at me!? (teenager voice) It's not my fault Lex Luther is holding all of the world's water for ransom! #FML!!!"

Such an attitude would hardly go over well with worldwide audiences. Intuitively, we expect more from our heroes – we demand total responsibility.

In fact, not only is Superman responsible for protecting the world, he's proactive, trying to protect it.

With hero status comes responsibility – a frightening consideration.

78

It's far easier to blame others and abdicate responsibility.

Assuming responsibility has many upsides. When you pick up responsibility, you must drop the excuses – blaming, b*tching, and complaining – which is liberating.

One of the most famous lines in superhero lore shares this very idea.

You may recall Uncle Ben's oft-repeated line, known as the Peter Parker Principle, as he cautions Peter Parker (Spiderman), **"With great power comes great responsibility."**

Let's quickly review and dissect the Monomyth's three main parts.

Understanding the Monomyth:
Part I. Departure:
Essentially, the hero is lost, stuck, frustrated, and spinning their wheels, or finds themself pushed or forced into a new environment.

As a quick aside, it's safe to say that more than half the people who find their way to The Habit Factor (app, book, or website) are seeking positive change. The common phrases they share include, "I feel stuck," "I feel like I'm just spinning my wheels," or "I'm not tapping into my full potential."

Here's another key point: This "stuck-ness" is a universal phenomenon; in psychological terms, it's "homeostasis": when one's needs and desires have been met. Thus, irony and paradox toy with our psyche, as it is our desire for comfort, balance, and equilibrium – a sense of "stasis" – we seek. Yet, to truly live and experience a full life and feel good about ourselves, we require challenges.

Extended periods of comfort bring about feelings of "stuck-ness" and a life devoid of fulfillment, perhaps even feelings of worthlessness or lack of meaning.

With Campbell's The Hero's Journey in mind, we see a pattern: Challenges create experiences and *stories*, and it's through these stories that we derive lessons and meaning.

Too much comfort saps our sense of purpose and self-worth. As the great surrealist artist Salvador Dali once put it, "There are some days when I think I'm going to die from an overdose of satisfaction."

Like the hero in the Hero's Journey, we seek something new and different.

"Hey, maybe I should sign up for a half-marathon."

But then we find ourselves caught between two conflicting impulses (and stories): the desire for comfort and "stasis" and the desire to grow and be challenged.

If we listen closely enough, we can hear the inner-story battle.

"A half-marathon!? Ha! You're so f*ing out of shape! Just think how dumb you'd look, not to mention the pain you'd be in! Plus, you do have that big, important report due at the end of the month. Nice idea, fat boy. You just don't have the time."

How's that for a script in which you are the HERO?

Big seller, right? Pretty compelling?

"Overweight workaholic has big, important report due, doesn't have time for himself or family."

News at 11 material, right?

There is no growth or lasting transformation without embracing the **HERO's** mindset. Notably, this is true for ALL goals.

The HERO's role and script happen to be conveniently framed by the H.E.R.O. acronym:

Hopeful: A better outcome or situation *is* possible. I *can* create my ideal future – do my best with what I have, one day at a time.

Empowered: I can make *it* happen! I am capable and confident.

Responsible: Nobody can do my pushups for me. Nobody is coming to save me.

Optimistic: Well, today's effort didn't go so well, but we learned something, and chances are good tomorrow, we'll fare even better!

Thus, I'm handing this to you. It's your checklist; consider it a filter through which to run your thinking – your various scripts and narratives.

Is your story, the one about your life and the world in which you live, as well as your present goals and challenges: (for starters)

Hopeful? ☐
Empowered? ☐
Responsible? ☐
Optimistic? ☐

With some awareness and observation, the fortunate few notice the counterargument.

"We're doing it this time! We've been talking about running a half-marathon for nearly a decade; the bullsh*t excuses are over. Time is up! There's never going to be a 'right' time! It's now or never!"

That's right, "*we*"!

The "we" is an acknowledgment of the battle between our two psyches – our attitudes of mind – the scripts playing in our head, forecasting how "things" will turn out.

Sigmund Freud, the Austrian-born neurologist and founder of psychoanalysis, spoke of three psyches: the id, ego, and super-ego. But when it comes to lasting transformation, performance, and achievement, there tend to be just two psyches in perpetual conflict.

You may simply recognize them as the yin and yang of personal achievement.

There's the **DP** (**Doubting Psyche**): ("No way you can pull that off!") Then there's the **HP** (**Hopeful Psyche**): ("Hey, give it a shot. If *they* can do it, I can do it. Let's go for it!")

Understanding these psyches leads us directly toward observing them and their related scripts.

Consider for a moment your biggest, most important goal right now. Which psyche do you hear?

Those who recognize the **HP** (Hopeful Psyche, the positive mental script) are fortunate. They still retain a sort of human barometer – a pressure gauge – that acknowledges their situation. "You're getting pretty soft,

Marty. Time to stop overthinking and take action. It's time to actually do some difficult things and challenge yourself!"

The hero ultimately recognizes this inescapable truth: There is no avoiding pain.

PAIN IS UNAVOIDABLE. It's inevitable! It's the suffering that is optional.

The late, great personal development icon Jim Rohn put it this way: "There are two great pains in life, discipline and regret."

That's the bad news.

Here's the good news: **You get to choose your pain.**

Select discipline, and the pain will be immediate but appears to diminish over time (largely because you become stronger). However, if you elect to avoid discipline, the pain lies dormant, growing in a deferred state until it morphs into the ultimate pain – the pain of regret!

The Two, Great and Unavoidable Pains of Life
Discipline & Regret

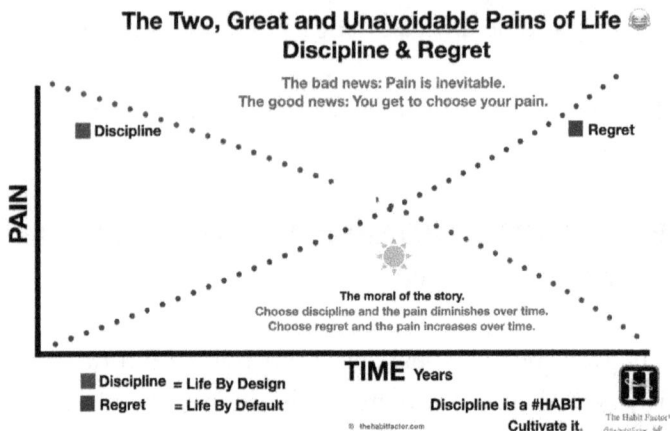

The Two, Great Unavoidable Pains of Life, courtesy of AutomaticGoals.com

In "The Ideal Road Not Taken," a research study by psychologist Tom Gilovich and a former Cornell graduate student, they discovered that people are more deeply haunted by regrets of failing to fulfill their goals, dreams, and aspirations than their obligations, responsibilities, and duties.

"Our most enduring regrets are the ones that stem from our failure to live up to our ideal selves," the report said.

"When we evaluate our lives, we think about whether we're heading toward our ideal selves, becoming the person we'd like to be. Those are the regrets that are going to stick with you because they are what you look at through the windshield of life," Gilovich said[19].

Pursuing your ideal self is the ultimate quest, and it's challenging.

Not pursuing your ideal self is easy and ultimately incredibly painful.

Challenge is the other vitamin "C." It's a vital human nutrient. Along with challenge comes pressure (a precursor to stress), which creates pain and discomfort, the "stuff" we (humans) are biologically wired to avoid.

It would be a grave mistake not to mention the ones who are *not* afforded the luxury to choose which challenges life throws their way.

There's my dear friend and perpetual inspiration, Klyn Elsbury, born with cystic fibrosis and given a prognosis not to live past 14.

Today, after over 70 hospitalizations and years where she spends 150 days in the hospital, Klyn has had every reason to throw up her hands and blame the world, the medical system, and everyone else for the sh*tty hand that she was dealt. Instead, she did the exact opposite, commandingly grabbing the captain's wheel – the helm – more days than not and steering herself toward a HERO's journey.

Today, at 34, she's a world-traveling professional speaker and bestselling author who has brilliantly managed to leverage her life experience from countless days in the hospital into practical tools and lessons other entrepreneurs can use.

That's a HERO's narrative!

Then there's my buddy, Shay Eskew. You may have heard his story. At age 8, he and his friend were accidentally set on fire by a 15-year-old neighbor.

You read that correctly. As the two boys attempted to help a neighbor clear out a yellowjacket's nest on their property, a teenage girl thought it'd be helpful to throw a match and gasoline at the nest, dousing the two boys and setting them ablaze.

Shortly after being hospitalized, Shay was told he'd never be competitive in sports again. He endured 40 surgeries, lost an ear, underwent numerous procedures to release his right arm that was physically melted to his body (he had to learn how to write left-handed to finish the third grade), wore plastic braces on his entire upper body for three years (torso, neck, and face), and battled the mental pain of being hospitalized for three months 500 miles from his family and friends. When he returned to school just two weeks after getting out of the hospital, he felt like an outcast. No one looked like him except villains in horror movies. Shay was picked on in school, bullied, and called "Freddy Krueger."

Further, due to the numerous surgeries and scarring over 65% of his body, Shay is unable to sweat from over one-third of his body. Even 40 years later, Shay is still undergoing surgeries. Despite all the hardship, Shay managed to craft a story in which he was the H.E.R.O.— not the victim.

Today, Shay is a world-class Ironman competitor ranked in the top 1% of Ironman athletes worldwide. He has competed in 44 Ironman events in 10 different countries spanning six continents, including 10 world championships.

So, where do you think you might run into (pardon the pun) a guy like Shay Eskew?

Turns out, he was one of the leaders of an adventure – an expedition of sorts – that I signed up for: The Rim2Rim2Rim Challenge at the Grand Canyon.

This was a 50-mile-plus expedition over a July 4 weekend in 100-plus-degree heat. We went from one side of the Grand Canyon down across the basin, slept a few hours, and then repeated the process.

In total, it was 15,000-plus feet of elevation hiking, all over a weekend.

Not that the event was an official race, but do you care to guess who finished first?

Shay.

That's correct. The guy who cannot perspire over 40% of his body was flying across the Grand Canyon and back in 100-plus-degree heat at an incomprehensible pace.

How is that possible?

Here's my theory: Shay's mentally tougher than most. And by most, I mean all of us.

He's been hardened by a lifetime of challenges.

Shay decided he would be bigger than his challenges and was very intentional about being the HERO of his own story. Precisely like Klyn Elsbury.

Hopeful   ☑
Empowered   ☑
Responsible   ☑
Optimistic   ☑

What if life doesn't hit us with a major setback or challenge, and we don't set challenging goals for ourselves?

Well, with no challenges in front of us for a prolonged period, we ultimately wither, weaken, and slowly die.

"Death!?"

Ha! That's a little dramatic, you say.

Perhaps, but not to worry, as those who are "dying" don't feel a thing. It's a lot like the fabled parable about the frog in a pot of slowly boiling water; its impending death is imperceptible, just one degree at a time, the frog never sensing its imminent demise.

The Hero's Journey provides universal appeal because it reveals our most profound personal questions and desires.

Could I do that?

Could I be the hero?

How might I respond if I were in their shoes?

We're captivated by the consideration and possibilities.

At the same time, we're enchanted by the struggle and personal growth story. Quietly and subconsciously, we desire such an adventure for ourselves.

Summary Part I: Either by choice or by chance, pressure, in the form of challenge, enters the story and catapults the hero out of "stasis." They must respond positively to grow and develop their character, skills, and confidence.

Part II. Initiation (and Trials)

With a clearly defined quest – a goal to be achieved or a purpose to pursue – the hero embarks upon a meaningful journey where, by its very nature, a multitude of trials, obstacles, and threats arise before them.

Key point (as covered in The Habit Factor): "In life, goals are NOT optional." Unfortunately, as far as I can recall, kids aren't taught this in school. Setting goals appears to be optional, something we can either elect to do or not.

You could argue, as some have, that getting an education is a goal, which it is. But teaching and learning about goals as subject matter – how and why they are essential and why habit serves as the primary driver of goal achievement – is not a class in and of itself, and it ought to be.

Not too long ago, I interviewed an artificial intelligence (AI) expert, Alex Bates, author of *Augmented Mind: AI, Humans, and the Superhuman Revolution.*[20] (Minute: 14:21)

Me: Is [artificial intelligence] not the ability for the computer to learn and teach itself?

Alex: Learning is a key part of it, but even broader than that, potentially, you can have intelligent behavior that was pre-programmed. **So, I think learning is fundamental, but artificial intelligence is a system [where] a lot of**

times they will include the term "goal-directed behavior," meaning it can accomplish goals, and sometimes there are challenges thrown its way, and sometimes it uses learning to accomplish those goals, and sometimes it doesn't.[21]

Please, reflect upon Alex's statement.

If artificial intelligence is goal-directed behavior, then what, I ask you (reader), is real intelligence?

Must not real intelligence also be goal-directed behavior?

In life, goals are NOT optional.
Goals are intelligence in action.

With each worthwhile goal comes a very special ingredient, almost like pre-loaded software: **pressure**.[22]

Worthy goals immediately present resistance, problems, challenges, and obstacles.

Has there ever been a great story without conflict? How compelling would a smooth sailing story be?

Similarly, each great story includes a hero with a clearly defined goal and purpose, one that produces immense pressure.

In pursuit of their goal, the hero encounters numerous trials; each tends to reveal less-than-heroic qualities, including fear, doubt, and insecurity, for starters.

The Hero's confidence is tested early and often.

Consider Luke fumbling around with the lightsaber or how Harry Potter nearly dies after a fall from a broomstick.

Once the hero crosses into the "unknown world," they accept that there is no turning back.

In *The Matrix*, Morpheus says to Neo, "This is your last chance. After this, there is no turning back. You take the blue pill, and the story ends. You wake up in your bed and believe whatever you want to believe. You take the red pill, you stay in Wonderland, and I show you how deep the rabbit hole goes."

By accepting the challenge, the hero must dig deep and, in so doing, discovers untapped talents and gifts. They're surprised to find how much stronger, tougher, smarter, and even more resilient they are! Latent talents, qualities, and resources reveal themselves only because they're tested by the journey's trials.

Further, the Hero's Journey assumes a spiritual aspect, as "dormant forces" avail themselves, including guides, angels, allies, mentors, and even simple good luck!

Picture Yoda agreeing to mentor Luke in *The Empire Strikes Back*, teaching him how to manage The Force.

Luke: Is the dark side stronger?

Yoda: No, no, no. Quicker, easier, more seductive.

"Quicker, easier, more seductive"?

Isn't that the opposite of the pressure and resistance that arise when pursuing worthwhile goals?

If you've read *The Habit Factor*, you will most likely recall Roz Savage's story from the book's Foreword.

Roz holds four Guinness World Records for ocean rowing, including being the first woman to row solo across the Atlantic, Pacific, and Indian oceans.

Roz and I connected after she blogged about tracking her habits using The Habit Factor app back in 2009. Curious, I learned more about her and her inspiring story and invited her to write *The Habit Factor* Foreword.

I could be wrong, but I'm guessing that rowing solo across the Pacific, Atlantic, and Indian oceans wasn't too quick, easy, or seductive.

Ha!

Speaking of oceans, recall the "dormant force" of a blue whale magically swallowing Nemo and Dory and delivering them to safety in Disney's classic *Finding Nemo*?

Summary Part II: With seemingly insurmountable obstacles at every turn, feelings of doubt and insecurity compound.

Yet, knowing there's no opportunity to return to the way things were or to quit, the hero must press forward and dig deep. In so doing, they discover that latent talents, skills, and forces miraculously come to their aid.

As the great Indian sage Patanjali stated, "When you are inspired by some great purpose, some extraordinary project, all your thoughts break their bonds. Your mind transcends limitations, your consciousness expands in every direction, and you find yourself in a new, great, and wonderful world.

Dormant forces, faculties, and talents become alive, and you discover yourself to be a greater person by far than you ever dreamed yourself to be."

Part III. Return:
The hero has accomplished the mission, and even if they didn't, it almost doesn't matter. As Mahatma Gandhi put it: "Glory lies in the attempt to reach one's goal and not in reaching it."

Thus, the journey itself has transformed the hero physically, mentally, and spiritually by virtue of their effort.

Once transformed, they are no longer the same person who initially ventured into an unknown and frightening world.

Whether by choice or chance doesn't matter; each discovers that they are better, stronger, faster, smarter, and more resilient because of their journey.

The final bonus – the biggest reward of all – is the *gift*.

The gift equates to the lessons the Hero gains from their journey. The gift is so valuable, so rewarding, and so paradigm-shifting that it must be shared with others.

Consider Luke's commitment to use the Force for good and protect the universe from the Dark Side by training other Jedis. Think of Neo in *The Matrix* vowing to save humanity or Elsa in *Frozen* coming to an understanding of how to control her powers for the greater good.

Upon the Hero's return, their purpose is elevated!

Most often, the hero's journey begins as a solo venture; it's about "ME." However, upon return, the hero's purpose is elevated; it becomes about "WE."

Once you appreciate the Hero's Journey as Campbell defined it, you'll see it everywhere. It's essential within the entertainment industry. Further, and more importantly, you'll notice it in real life.

You'll see the Hero's Journey among your friends and loved ones, those who've challenged themselves (by choice or by chance), who've leaned into and faced the wind, jumped headfirst into the abyss; frightened and confused, only to return later different, more confident, and complete – better!

Transformed, they possess the "gift" – a reward they're compelled to share with others.

You'll see these stories playing out everywhere.

You'll notice them each time you challenge yourself, respond to a difficulty, and develop new skills and habits. While those efforts may not be as glorious or heroic as Luke Skywalker destroying the Dark Side, there is a pattern, and it's notable.

It's easy to see the Hero's Journey storyline play out at various points in my life, whether it was a "failed" entrepreneurial venture, a quest to complete the Catalina Classic, Ironman events, or pursuing big-wave tow-in surfing. Each produced enormous pressure, resistance, anxiety, pain, doubt, and uncertainty.

Even when writing these books, the same pattern emerges: confusion, chaos, doubt, struggle, and then, finally, some order. And, with some good fortune, value emerges.

It becomes clear: The journey itself is the reward – the "gift." That's the story to be shared.

Despite all the hardships thrown a Hero's way, a peculiar hunger grows: the desire to learn and explore your limits and potential. Notice how Roz was only getting started *after* she completed her Atlantic Ocean row.

DEPRESSED

"There is no way to happiness.
Happiness is the way."
~ Thich Nhat Hanh

I'd just missed a third week of work. Still confined to my bed, I rolled over to my side, possessed by an eerie self-awareness. "What the hell is going on here? Do you really want to die like this?"

The year was 1992. I was 24 and had visited several doctors, but none were able to find a thing wrong with me, even though my weight had dropped to a feeble 134 pounds. (For context, as a senior in high school, I wrestled at 156 pounds.)

"Do you really want to die like this?" I repeated the question.

I wasn't being dramatic. I sensed my condition was going to deteriorate quickly.

The question itself, coupled with my state of awareness, caught me off guard. Even as I share this story, nearly 30 years later, I have no idea why that morning (the 26th morning) was any different from the prior 25, but something clicked.

In hindsight, the story is even more peculiar since, at the time, from the outside looking in, I had the proverbial world by the tail.

Leading up to my confinement, I had a great deal going for me. I'd just returned from a second backpacking trip around Europe within two years, this time with my girlfriend. I had my health, and I was surfing up to six times a week. I was a recent graduate of SDSU; I had a solid job and was doing my own computer consulting on the side. The biggest bonus of all: I lived at the beach.

Yet, the undeniable truth – the truth that no person suggested or doctor diagnosed: I was clinically depressed.

I had "everything," yet all that consumed my mind – my thinking from one hour to the next, day after day, for months leading up to being bedridden, was, "What the F*CK is going on with this horrific world!?"

I was fixated upon the world's problems – the injustices, illness, disease, poverty, starvation, sickness, racism, and overpopulation, not to mention the wars and conflict around the world at the time, atrocities in the Serbia/Yugoslav wars, and the Gulf War. Throw in the mess that is factory farming, global warming, pollution, mass shootings, and over-consumption – the disheartening list seemed to grow longer by the day.

To boot, irony had its way with me. A recent graduate from the fun farm that was SDSU (at least in the early '90s), I had great ambitions. I was prepared to field multiple job offers from leading ad agencies dying to place me as their next prodigious Art Director.

Yet, two years removed from college, I was the "Desktop Design Manager." You know, "paying my dues" with important work like designing flyers. Think babysitters for hire, missing pets, and homes for sale. (This was a store very similar to Kinkos, or as it's known today, FedEx/Kinkos.)

I just laid there on my side, lethargic, numb, and repeated the question, "Do you really want to die like this?" Then, entirely out of the blue, the gut-punch question: **"Is this how you want to be remembered?"**

"No!"

I was as surprised by my response as the question itself; it was nothing short of a revelation. The idea of dying and being remembered at all (at 24) was a novel concept. But now, faced with the reality of a dangerously different physical, emotional, and mental condition, that was *the* question that surprisingly surfaced.

The notion that my life could culminate in this: a frail, scared, and scarred 24-year-old unable to navigate his way through a brutally tough world full of problems, sent a disruptive jolt throughout my body.

"No more!" I seconded the motion, this time, a more spirited affirmation.

"Are you sure?" I challenged myself. "Really?"

"Yes!"

As the saying goes, "I was sick and tired of being sick and tired." It may have taken 26 days, but in an instant, I flipped the script. The logic that followed was crystal clear: If I was certain that I needed to get healthy and didn't want to be remembered like this, "things" needed to change in a hurry.

Aristotle reportedly described wisdom as, "The equal measure of experience plus reflection."

Looking back, it's easy to see that while I had "everything," I lacked the most elemental and crucial of all things: **control of my thinking**.

I needed to grab the steering wheel; the responsibility was mine alone. "No one saves us but ourselves. No one can, and no one may. We ourselves must walk the path." This gem from the Dhammapada was an insight that would have made little sense to me at the time. Now, the message is immeasurably important.

I ran my vessel aground, and there was only one way to get back to safe and peaceful waters. It was clear that I had to direct my thinking with intention. I had to set my sights on a new destination.

I needed to change my story.

Jim Rohn, the late, great motivational speaker, loved to put it this way: "You cannot change your destination overnight, but you can change your direction."

By declaring "No more!" my direction changed instantly, and unknown to me then, so did my story.

"Begin with the end in mind" is a brilliant maxim popularized by the wonderful work of Dr. Stephen Covey in his bestseller, *The Seven Habits of Highly Effective People*. To "begin with the end in mind," Dr. Covey would emphasize, is the first of the seven habits one should cultivate to be an effective human.

There is no greater "end" than our own demise. So, if "beginning with the end in mind" is important (and it is), it stands to reason that the most crucial mental exercise we can all perform is our own "END" *story*.

In the Foreword of *The Habit Factor*, Roz Savage shares an exercise that altered her life story *forever*. Recall that Roz holds four Guinness World Records for ocean rowing, including being the first woman to row solo across the Atlantic, Pacific, and Indian oceans.

You may ask, "What the f*ck could possibly compel a person (any person) to row across three oceans solo?"

Not surprisingly, **Roz began with the end in mind**!

In the Foreword, she wrote:

I had reached a point of absolute desperation. I started seeking answers to some big questions. What did my life mean? What was the point of being me? But the question that really turned my life upside down was when I considered how I might be remembered. I sat down and wrote two versions of my own obituary – the one I wanted and the one I was headed for. They were very different; I realized I had to make some big changes if I was going to look back upon my life and be proud of my legacy.

Her story reveals what changed everything: She contemplated how she might be remembered.

Once again, not coincidentally, that is the very same question I encountered in my depressed state. The question that "sent a disruptive jolt throughout my body" and left an indelible mark upon my consciousness – a question that's still with me to this day.

It's important to point out the obvious: Roz proactively wrote her story.

We tend to think of stories as past tense and passive, the *result* of an experience, event, or even a life that happened to us. It's essential to recognize that our (life) stories can, and often should, be written *first*.

Those we admire most – the greats, our heroes, the ones we revere and put on a pedestal – did not sit around wondering what life had in store for them. Instead, they proactively and intentionally grabbed the pencil and paper and wrote their own story in advance.

Even if it wasn't literal writing, as Roz did, it was mental imaging – a visioning exercise. They pictured where they wanted to go with their lives, even if they had no clue if or how they might get there.

They charted a course – an ideal destination – they grabbed the steering wheel and assumed responsibility.

Our heroes scripted an ideal life, and then life scripted their story.

They had no idea how their story might unfold or even end, but they did have a target – *an ideal to pursue*. They believed in the cause and direction and, despite doubt and uncertainty, charted the course and acted purposefully.

Each of our heroes was courageous enough to take the first step – to envision an ideal destination and begin their quest.

It's almost as if our subconscious mind waits patiently, and in the still and quiet moments, asks, "So, what's it gonna be? What's your story?"

At 24, it never occurred to me that being bedridden for so long was due to months, perhaps years, of errant, uncontrolled thought.

In *As a Man Thinketh,* James Allen cautions, "Keep your hand firmly upon the helm of thought... Self-control is strength; Right Thought is mastery; Calmness is power."

Recall William James's observation from the Preface – how one's body and mind are inextricably linked – and it becomes inescapable: My habitual focus on negatives – the world's problems – coupled with my inability to come close to my professional aspirations at such a young age, were responsible for my physiological and physical deterioration.

I laid on my side and started to look around my room, searching – the same room I'd lived in for a couple of years and was now confined to for the last 25 days.

As I share this now, I'm bewildered by how the book was even on my bookshelf, let alone why it was *this* book that caught my attention.

The Power of Positive Thinking, by Norman Vincent Peale, sat where it must have sat for months or even years without notice; it was a book I'd never touched.

Still on my side, fatigued, not even sitting up, I gradually reached for it. I rolled over to my back and randomly opened it. After so many years, I have no recollection of the chapter or passage I first read, but I do recall the underlying message.

"Change your thoughts, and you change your world."

This was an unusual idea for me at that time. "Could it be that straightforward? Has my thinking been so 'wrong' for so long?" Particularly as it related to my outlook on the world at large.

Einstein reportedly said, "The most important decision we make is whether we believe we live in a friendly or hostile universe."

His statement makes perfect sense (as you might expect; he *is* Einstein). From that simple question, a decision is rendered, and one's beliefs (stories) and actions spill forward.

I touched upon Einstein's statement in *The Pressure Paradox,* so I won't repeat too much here. But it's safe to say that there's ample evidence to support the idea of *both* a friendly and a hostile universe.

If you believe the universe is "hostile," recall the 3 Circles and how the Behavior Echo-System operates – how our feelings, emotions, actions, behaviors, habits, and skills are impacted, influencing our results and environment.

So, should you be guided by a deep, underlying belief in a hostile world, you're likely to develop noticeable and subliminal feelings of anger, fear, and even hopelessness.

Participation time.

Do you think this is a friendly or hostile universe?

What's your answer?

Thoreau handled the same dilemma a bit less binary and far more literally: "It's not what you look at that matters," he insisted. **"It's what you *see*."**

Even though Thoreau made his statement 100-plus years before science discovered the RAS (Reticular Activating System), he clearly understood its significance.

In a world full of *infinite* data points and sensations, the RAS helps us narrow our focus to those "things" (data points) that we deem important, interesting, and, curiously enough, *support our beliefs.*

For instance, during the Covid-19 Pandemic, there's the story about how everyone is an idiot who doesn't wear a mask, given there is so much evidence to support mask-wearing to stop the spread of airborne viruses.

At the very same time, it's the same RAS in another person that supports a perfectly contradictory story with "ample evidence" that masks do "nothing."

What's the difference?

I would suggest to you it's this:

It's not what you look at that matters; it's what you see.

The RAS helps us explain why, when we learn a new word or read a new book, we tend to *notice* the word or the book everywhere. Or, when you buy your daughter a white VW Beetle convertible, you notice white VW convertibles everywhere.

Unbeknownst to me, at 24, my RAS had gone haywire. For years leading up to my illness, my senses and emotions were overwhelmed by a world of "chaos," disorder, and injustice. All I "looked at" and "saw" were the negatives. I failed to "see" *opportunity*.

You may be saying, "What the hell are you talking about? Opportunity? Are you crazy!? Where is opportunity in disease, famine, war, factory farming, and global pollution, for starters?"

Here's my response to *your* question.

You tell me.

What do you *see*?

I failed to appreciate *myself as part of the solution*, not just part of the problem.

What I "looked" at and what I "saw" did *not* diverge. I needed to recognize that with intention and focus, I could, for lack of a better word, bring "light" to where there was darkness – certainly far more helpful than just bringing more darkness and negativity.

I was "looking at" and "seeing" the same thing: hopelessness.

Thoreau's point: We can *choose* to see hope where things appear hopeless. We can *choose* to be empowered where things appear to be difficult. We could *choose* to be responsible and take ownership – to help solve the problems we notice. And we could *choose* to be optimistic and see opportunity within each crisis.

We *can* and should be the **HERO** of any crises (stories) that attract our attention, whether they're personal, civic, national, international, or even global – those problems that call to your heart and soul.

Tragically, there is no shortage of crises throughout the world, and I've heard it argued that is precisely why there are so many people. Isn't responding to crises with hope and fashioning opportunities what the most innovative entrepreneurs and companies do?

Take Dutch artist Daan Roosegaarde, who invented a "Tower that sucks up smog and produces diamonds" after visiting Beijing and looking out his window, unable to see the city because the smog was so thick.

Or, David Katz, founder of The Plastic Bank, who came to realize that he could develop an ethical recycling ecosystem around the world, within coastal communities, to reprocess gathered plastics for reintroduction into the global manufacturing supply chain. Collectors then receive a premium for the materials to buy basic family necessities such as groceries, school tuition, and health insurance.

Or, consider the company Beyond Meat, which set a record-breaking IPO with its mission to redefine what meat can be and how its efforts can greatly diminish the effects of factory farming and pollution and even mitigate our health crises.

"In the midst of *every* crisis lies great opportunity," Einstein assured us.

In short: Depending on how we *see* our crises and challenges – personal, communal, or otherwise – we can choose to craft a different *ending* and, with it, a more positive story.

I rolled over to my other side, now facing the door.

Twenty-six days later.

I sat up, staring at the door.

"When you get up in the morning," Norman Vincent Peale reassured us, "you have two choices – either to be happy or to be unhappy. Just choose to be happy."

I lifted my head and took a deep breath, and *thought*, today is going to be better.

I felt lighter.

I chose happiness.

WORRIES

*"I've had a lot of worries in my life,
most of which never happened."*
~Mark Twain

"Why would you write a book and not put your name on it?" Scotty persisted. *The 3 C's of SuCCCess* was selling well enough at the time to terrify me (2008).[23]

I had just confided in my Entrepreneur's Organization forum, "The Rock," that my first book was "live" and currently selling. It was a self-help and personal development book entitled *The 3 C's of SuCCCess*.

If you can believe it, I was scared. I was afraid the book would do too well and that I wouldn't be able to hide.

That was my big worry.

To make matters worse, I wasn't honest with myself; I wasn't acknowledging or even aware that *this* was my big worry.

It seems comical now.

I wrote *The 3 C's of SuCCCess* under the pen name of Mitch W. Steel. How and why *that* became my pen name is a story for another day.

My excuse for having a pen name, my external narrative, was created to justify and hide my internal fear – that the book would be a huge sales success and I would be "outed" as a know-nothing, struggling entrepreneur in his early thirties.

"Who the f*ck are you to be writing about success? Whether it has three C's or 35 C's?!"

"You don't know sh*t!"

I was calling myself out.

Beautifully conflicted.

I had never written or published anything, and I certainly had no understanding of my capacity or capability as a writer.

My identity story – my self-concept – did not include author.[20]

The short story, one I can see clearly now, is that I didn't see myself as an expert, even though I'd just spent a few years writing as well as teaching many of these ideas. Further, I'd volunteered to teach for the non-profit organization Junior Achievement, which places "business leaders" into local classrooms, teaching topics such as success.

When the program counselor asked if I'd be interested in teaching "Success Skills," a 10-week program to high school students, I was struck by the serendipity and jumped at the opportunity. I was already captivated by the subject of success and deep into writing *The 3 C's*.

"Scotty," I reassured my befuddled friend. "These ideas are much bigger than any *one* person. I'm not interested in taking credit, just helping people."

---

[20] More on character and identity in the next section.

Even crazier, I believed it.

It was my truth.

It was my story.

I recall him shaking his head, probably muttering to himself, "What a dummy! This guy doesn't even want to take credit for a book he spent a lot of time writing, and it's a bestseller."[21]

I fully subscribed to my justification of anonymity in the interest of promoting *ideas* and not people. To be clear, the person I had no interest in pushing or promoting was me.

Not that it necessarily applies here, but I'm reminded of this Charles Bukowski quote: "The problem with the world is that the intelligent people are full of doubts, while the stupid ones are full of confidence."

The book was as much a creative calling as it was a way to get the ideas out of my head. By writing about these "success" theories, I thought I would be free.

But to publish them? *Under my name!?*

No, thank you.

I was so filled with doubt and uncertainty that I'm not sure it was a conscious decision. Using a pen name was more of an unconscious directive.

Better still, I had a terrific story to justify my decision.

After all, I explained to anyone who asked, "Authors do it all the time. Ben Franklin wrote and published *Poor Richard's Almanac* at the age of 26 under the name Richard Saunders."

---

[21] Amazon bestseller, 2008–2012, in its category.

Now, however, it's crystal clear that using a pen name was merely an effort to disguise my unconscious fear.

I would later learn that *this* is an important and fundamental concept within human psychology:

Humans are self-justifying creatures.

We (humans) justify our decisions and actions, consciously and unconsciously, *as often as possible*. And, perhaps not surprisingly, this habit extends toward our poorest decisions and actions, including even self-destructive or harmful actions toward others.

To be clear, our self-justification takes the form of story.

Consciously, and more often unconsciously, we craft and adopt clever little narratives, all done to avoid looking stupid.

The truth is nobody ever wants to appear dumb. So, when we mess up, we justify it with a good story. These are a couple of *my* recent favorites:

"I wouldn't have run that stop sign if that overgrown tree branch wasn't blocking part of the sign."

"I wouldn't have locked the keys in the car if you didn't park the car on the curb for the entire weekend!"

Now you're invited to play along. Have a go:

"I wouldn't have said/texted/emailed ___X___ if you didn't say/text/email ___Y___."

This self-justification doesn't need to be an elaborate story. But, make no mistake, it's a story.

It's a means to justify our actions and do our very best to keep our *self-image* intact. [22]

Being wrong challenges our ego, self-image, and intellect. It's as if we're afraid the perception will be, "Hey, world! Check me out; I'm a f*cking idiot!"

So, rather than admit a mistake and quickly apologize, more often than not, we'll do our best to rationalize the error with a good story.

Rationalize.

Rational. Lies.

It's easy to do; after all, it's *our* story.

We back our actions, biases, beliefs, values, and ideas, and then we justify the f*ck out of them.

Self-justification is a raw and real part of human nature, and that is precisely what psychology has labeled it.

Self-justification.

I encourage you to visit any prison in any part of the world; most, if not all, prisoners will tell you their *side of the story*, the one that *justifies* their actions.

You'll hear a story about how and why they were "right" and almost certainly why the system, circumstances, and situation "wronged" them.

For example, I know a guy whose father served nearly a decade for trafficking marijuana in the '90s.

---

[22] More on self-image in the next section.

Think about how easy it is for him to justify his actions, given the *current* laws and regulations!

Do you not think he has a good story about how messed up the laws *were* relative to marijuana and how all his misfortune – including 10 years of his life spent in prison – is a *crime against him*? And, when it comes to his desire to have the felony expunged from his record, arguably, his story has merit.

The 3 C's of SuCCCes was my original foray into expressing a handful of "self-help" ideas with the deep belief that they could help people.

Yet, ironically, there I was, hiding behind a pen name, filled with doubt and insecurity.

Me? Author? Ha!

Let alone an author about success principles.

No way! Not a chance!

Time to hide.

Nikki C   Mon, Nov 28, 2011, 8:55 AM
to me

Dear Mitch, is it possible to purchase 30 - 50 paperbacks of the 3Cs to success at a discount. I cannot buy more than 7 at a time from amazon, I loved the book and would like to gift them to my partners. If so what would the price be.

Thank you,

nikki c

Nikki C   Sun, Dec 4, 2011, 8:36 PM
to me

I would love to order 45 books at 8.99 each. Please send to Nikki C
S. D   Los Angeles, CA 90   My phone number is 541-   -   I am
traveling tomorrow and will be in U.S. until afternoon, if you could leave me a
message as to where to call you to give you a credit card number on Monday,
the 5th before I am out of the country that would be great. Would love to have
the books in before xmas if at all possible (maybe by the 20th?) If that is
impossible I still want to order.

Nassim A   Wed, Feb 3, 2010, 12:35 AM
to me

Hello,

I need to send you money for two copies for your book. Happy readers
they've made! If paypal, do i just use your email address ?

Nassim A.
Thanks

Greg S   Tue, Nov 26, 2013, 5:35 PM
to me

HI Mitch

Thanks so much. It's nice that you've honoured the purchase after so
long. Very much appreciated, and by a quick glance at the material, I'm
sure it will be forever useful.
Many thanks also for the P.E.T. booklet. Can't wait to get started!

You've made my day Mitch, and it's only just begun.

☺

Lauri S   Fri, Jan 14, 2011, 1:24 AM
to MitchWSteel

Hello Mitch,

thank you for you web site (and now the book) which have provided me many insights and help
in managing my life.

Sad?

Funny?

Ironic?

"I'll take D, Bob, for all of the above!"

The real prize, the reason I'm even sharing *this story*, is two-fold. First, it's a perfect illustration of just how "off" our limiting beliefs, doubts, and fears can be, not to mention how subversive such storytelling is to our creative nature. Leonardo da Vinci, one of the most prolific creators in history, put it like this: "The greatest deception men suffer is from their own opinions."

Second, it's a perfect segue into the following, dare I say, most important section of *this book*: "The Stories That Really F*cking Matter."

Think about that concept deeply before you arrive there.

If everything is a f*cking story, what do you think are the stories that really matter?

Don't jump ahead.

While you ponder that question, please recognize this and the very next chapter as wonderful, albeit painful, stories that illustrate the challenges that are likely to arise when there is *incongruency* and *misalignment* between our goals and desires and our stories.

FAILURE

Pain: a seed for strength
Disappointment: a seed for patience
Rejection: a seed for resilience
Failure: a seed for success

Darren Hardy is a prodigy – maybe *the* prodigy – a perpetual student of an enormous amount of personal development study as well as a bestselling author of *The Compound Effect, Entrepreneur Roller Coaster, Living Your Best Year Ever*, and more.

I'm not saying Darren isn't human; I'm saying he's likely more refined than most.

In short, Darren has devoted much of his life to improving himself and helping others do the same.

The date was September 12, 2012, and Darren and I had just wrapped up a fairly disastrous interview. At the time, Darren was the publisher of Success.com, and I had been invited to do an audio interview about *The Habit Factor.*

He was in Florida (I think), and I was in the Success.com studio in San Diego.

I walked out of the studio shaking my head, overwhelmed by a sense of confusion and guilt, peppered with a bit of humiliation.

"What the f*ck was that? What just happened!?"

"You completely f*cked up! You just wasted everyone's time!" I drove back to my office, numb.

It all started with a tweet a couple of months prior. "We're trying to get ahold of Martin Grunburg for an interview." It came via one of Success.com's personnel and was directed to me.

"Holy sh*t! Sweeeeet!"

I remember thinking just how inevitable it all was – more interviews, not just Success.com, but many others, soon to follow.

On the one hand, cocky, on the other hand (soon to be discovered), fearful and confused.

#ComplicatedAF!

At the time, The Habit Factor had gained substantial momentum (app and book), and there had been notable coverage, all without solicitation: New York Times, C-Net, Lifehacker.com, etc.

So, dear reader, here's where the story gets a little, or a lot, weird.

In personal development literature and behavior psychology, much is written about the "The fear of success," "success rejection phenomenon," or "imposter syndrome."

If you haven't heard of any of these "conditions," which are all somewhat related, they look and sound something like this: You have a prevalent and often unconscious fear of succeeding to the point where you might find yourself sabotaging events, circumstances, and efforts subconsciously and consciously, and you have a hard time understanding why.

Important point: The fear is related to the consequences you believe will impact your life when you achieve "success." In other words, the fear is directly related to the story you've crafted about how "success" will change your future.

You read that correctly.

The fear is related to the challenges you think will occur when you realize success.

All of it, story.

***

Sidenote: The Habit Factor and The Habits 2 Goals podcast tend to attract a seemingly disproportionate amount of people with advanced education degrees (Ph.Ds. and masters). I may finally understand why: These people tend to overthink habitually.

Overthinking is often exhaustive, incongruent storytelling.

In short, an enormous amount of time and energy is wasted on imaginative, unsupportive, and often irrelevant stories standing between overthinkers and their goals and ideals.

***

In my case, my overthinking story sounded a lot like this: "Oh, sh*t! Here we go. The Habit Factor is getting out of control. You're going to become a mega-bestselling author and travel the world constantly!" (Just a year prior, I had been invited to present at TEDx Alain in the United Arab Emirates.)

My worries intensified. "Your new scheduling demands will completely upend life as you know it!" The story continued.

"You can kiss surfing four-plus days a week goodbye. Same with golfing with your buddies. Your newfound author 'fame' will complicate the f*ck out of your life."

"And…!"

Wait…there's more?

"Yes! You idiot! Don't forget about your business partners! You know, the guys, along with their wives, with whom you've shed blood, sweat, and tears for the last decade and a half!" (It was an IT services business unrelated to The Habit Factor.) "How do you think they are going to react when you're out of town, no longer contributing time or energy to the company that you all founded together so many years ago!?"

In short, I was playing a strange game of chess, anticipating future moves and consequences while trying to preserve and protect all that was good, near, and dear in my life at the moment.

In retrospect – the fabulously painful part – they were consequences that did not yet exist.

Incredibly, the fear had begun to chip away at my drive to promote The Habit Factor, particularly if it came at the cost of my most important relationships and the current lifestyle I loved so much.

For a bit more context: The Habit Factor was a side-project – a creative, philosophical pursuit. I'd never intended to become "author/speaker guy," an identity I had no story for. If I had an identity story, it was one I was familiar and comfortable with: entrepreneur and surfer guy.

To tie this story to the "Meaning" chapter and Campbell's "Hero's Journey," it's easy to see how I was doing my part to refuse "The Call."

The "Unknown World" was knocking on my door, and I much preferred the "Known World."

By 2012, The Habit Factor book (and app) had taken on a life of their own, and with the Success.com interview looming (tough to be more literal than that – Success.com), the countdown to my life's derailment had begun.

Tick. Tock.

My subconscious went to work and drove strange decisions, actions, and behaviors, including delaying, deferring, and even refusing new potential business partners and investors all interested in promoting The Habit Factor.

Family, existing partners, and friends (my most important relationships) vs. The Habit Factor's growth and success.

Pick-'em, Marty.

Buried even deeper, and almost certainly the strongest deterrent of all, was my fear of not being around for my daughters as they grew up (aged 8 and 10 at the time). The idea of not seeing or playing with them, not surfing with them, or coaching their soccer practices and games, was unacceptable.

No way.

It wasn't as though I didn't travel. I had my fair share of travel and surf jaunts to Tahiti, Peru, Panama, Indonesia, Mexico, Nicaragua, etc. Still, the idea of traveling for business, full-time, to earn a living, and at the cost of not being around for my daughters – apparently, I wasn't too interested.

In retrospect, to be fair to me (MG v.2012), I had ammo; there was plenty of evidence (justification) to warrant my story.

I'd witnessed many "successful" people, particularly those in the personal development and speaking industries, chase money, "success," fame, etc., at the cost of family time. The more I was sucked into that world, the more dysfunction I noticed, including divorces and absentee fathers.

Since I was unaware of my "stories" conflict, I didn't recognize that I'd presented myself with a horrible, false dichotomy.

It didn't have to be one or the other. It could have been both.

No awareness, no accurate thinking.
Sometimes luggage, sometimes baggage.

The key to knowing the difference is first to recognize the stories – to assess and take inventory (as discussed in the Prologue), to notice the feelings, emotions, and actions, particularly if they don't seem to lead you where you think you want to go.

EVERYTHING Is A F*cking Story

Those are the clues, the triggers I should have recognized to understand my behaviors. I had no appreciation for many of these ideas: that we think predominantly in terms of story, and these stories will direct and influence our decisions, behaviors, and actions.

Thus, the winner of my fallacious death match was predefined. It was just a matter of time.

Now, given everything you've read herein about self-justification and rationalization, it'd be fair to comment, "Hey, isn't this just some bullsh*t, self-justification story MG is using to validate an interview gone horribly wrong?"

That is entirely possible.

However, there is more to the story (smile), far more relative to processing and using "failures" to one's advantage. There are even more important questions to ask.

"If everything is a f*cking story, and all of our stories tend to justify our actions and behaviors, how does one know *which* story to trust – to lean on?"

"How does one know which story they should subscribe to?"

Excellent questions.

You are encouraged to ponder them deeply.

It turns out that experience-sharing (stories – part of Gestalt protocol, which is used within Gestalt therapy) – is designed to help participants learn from their own as well as others' experiences.

Advice is cheap. Anyone can give advice, and most people do. Unfortunately, the self-help world is saturated with advice.

Experience-shares, though, and personal stories typically come with a cost. Often, the cost includes hard-won lessons by a person who's failed and discovered a way to turn their mess into their message.

It just so happens that *The Habit Factor* and *The Pressure Paradox* are both packed with my experience-shares, as is *The 3C's of SuCCCess*. And, it turns out, this book provides even more "hard-won lessons."

Further, you ought to know there is a form of therapy called "narrative therapy."[23]

In short, narrative therapy is a form of counseling that helps people to recognize they are separate from their problems. This is done by assessing their stories.

Narratives.

Allegories.

Parables.

A wise man learns more from a fool than a fool from a wise man.

How? By observing his experiences.

No matter how close you are to religion, chances are excellent that you haven't witnessed any of the stories recited in your holy book. *Instead, they are all stories.*

---

[23] I have no direct experience with narrative therapy.

Recall Banzan at the opening of this book, walking through the butcher shop as he overhears a conversation between a customer and the butcher.

That's a story.

So, my experience-share here, my story, while necessary, is done with reluctance.

As I wrote this chapter and pondered these questions, *one* key question kept surfacing, "Is there a source – an origin story – relative to my 'success rejection syndrome'"?

If so, where or when did it arise?

Is it one story, two stories…10 stories?

Cosmic-*Twilight-Zone*-esque music.

We enter another dimension…

I'm 8ish years old; it's halftime at my soccer game, *I* have scored four goals, and we're up 4-0. The coach, parents, and team are all elated!

Our team is winning big time.

My grandfather, "Morfar," is visiting from Sweden. He's a huge "football" fan, and he's attending the game. Everyone is excited – or so I think. As I look around, I notice something strange – something I may have carried with me for decades.

Not everyone is happy.

Not everyone is excited.

Instead, a handful of kids on my team look dejected, deflated, and unhappy.

At that age, it's tough not to pick up on the facial expressions, body language, and other kids' vibes and emotions.

During the half, I distinctly recall other parents pointing at me while talking or even yelling at their child. Pointing. I see it like it was yesterday – I can hear it, "Come on, Johnny! Play like *him*." "Play like Martin!"

To be clear, this is *not* self-praise. It's actually the opposite. This little nugget of a memory/story may have haunted me for a while. And, by a while, I mean decades.

[Me, talking to myself:]
"Shut up!? You mean decades of behavior could be driven by one dumb little story?
"Is that even possible?"
I don't know!?
Is it possible to fake decades of decisions, actions, behaviors, and habits?"
Is it possible to fake one's values?
To be clear, I've never shared this story anywhere, anytime, with anyone.
So, yes, I'm going deep.

Back to the soccer game:
You'd think a performance like that would make me feel terrific. Four goals by halftime? "Play like Martin!"
Apparently, I felt something else.
Guilt? Shame? Embarrassment?
Did I have to score all those goals?
Could I not have passed the ball?

It occurred to me that I'd stolen the spotlight from the other kids.

Now, to be clear, I'm nearly certain such a childhood, competitive athletic experience is *not uncommon*; chances are good there are likely thousands, perhaps millions, of children who've experienced something similar.

(By the way, that's the sort of awareness that might've been helpful, oh, I don't know, anytime over the last 30-plus years. LOL.)

Back to the game:

On the one hand, I loved the achievement and the feeling of success. However, I began to sense something else. Alienation?

Was "success" coming at a cost?

Was the cost the other kids' enjoyment and perhaps even their self-worth?

Did they hate me because I was a show-off?

At 8ish years old, are these not real concerns?

It wasn't until I arrived at this chapter and started unearthing – roaming through the ashes – a lifetime of setbacks, disappointments, and "failures" that I began seeking some answers.

Why have things gone "sideways" when they did?

Why, so often, when the spotlight was on me, did I revert to the humble, quiet, "hate-the-spotlight guy"?

Did I suffer from "success rejection" syndrome?

Why did I turn away multiple new business ventures looking to invest and grow The Habit Factor?

The questions I asked myself continued.

Why did you become a camp counselor (ages 16–22)?

Why were you a lifeguard and swim instructor teaching kids at the La Jolla YMCA during my summers at SDSU?

Why did you become a volunteer mentor and Big Brother for Big Brothers Big Sisters of San Diego? (Today, my "little" brother is 34.)

Why was your first entrepreneurial venture (with investors) Kreative Kids Computer Camp? A computer camp dedicated to teaching kids about computers and making it FUN! (1994-1997)

Why did you serve on the Board of Directors of Big Brothers Big Sisters of San Diego for more than 10 years?

Why did you become a volunteer teacher for Junior Achievement, teaching their 10-week Success Skills course to socially disadvantaged youths throughout San Diego?

Why did you become the middle school soccer coach for your daughters' teams for four years?

Why have you been the mentoring chair for Entrepreneurs Organization?

Why did you moderate and coach Entrepreneur Organization's Accelerator Forums?[24]

Why the f*ck do you write these personal development books!?

---

[24] EOA forums exist to help fellow entrepreneurs grow their companies' revenue upward of $1 million.

What's the common, underlying *theme* in the above roles? Is there a pattern?

Apparently, it was – and still is – teaching, coaching, guiding, and serving others.

My coaching style? Be tough on the "stars" – give them *less* attention. This should have been my first clue. I was naturally inclined to work with the self-conscious kids who doubted their abilities – to build them up.

Again, to be as clear as possible: My little story-share is to demonstrate how you can learn from past stories and present behaviors. It turns out that my guiding values and half of my life's decisions, actions, and behaviors are almost certainly the result of experiences (stories) that have impacted my psyche, for better or worse, and I can almost guarantee the same for you.

There is, of course, more to the story. There's an additional, essential part of the process to help you observe, learn from, and discover a better way through your own story analysis and inventory system. This story tees up that process.

We'll address much of this when we arrive at the "Why?" chapter in the next section, "The Stories that Really Freakin' Matter." The rest of the process can be found in the "Application" section.

***

Postscript: Nearly two years after the Success.com fiasco, I finally shared this story over lunch with a fellow entrepreneur who'd recently sold his company and was moving to Hawaii.

I confessed, "It [the interview] was sooo bad…a total mess. I'm so bummed I let Darren down and wasted his time." I was still shaking my head in nearly the identical, confused manner as when I left the studio that day. Here I was, almost two years later, still licking my wounds and trying to understand how that could happen.

My buddy's response was instant. "It's all good, Martin," he said with a smile and sipped his beer. "It was probably meant to happen. Think about it this way: You needed that to happen, so it doesn't when you're doing even bigger interviews on larger platforms."

And with that, I should have appreciated the art of storytelling.

I wasn't ready.

HOPE

"Hope is a waking dream."
~ Aristotle

Jimmy sat across from me as we attempted to enjoy our post-golf beers. He was dejected – as depressed as I'd ever seen. To make matters worse, he had just played a terrible round of golf, which was entirely understandable given the bad news. "It's *all* f*cking ruined," he muttered. "I'm a failure."

He kept going. "I'm divorced, nearly bankrupt, and now, the one thing – the *one* f*cking thing I had going." He was shouting at this point. "This! This new f*cking venture, and *IT* just went up in smoke!"

Slamming his fist on the table, he declared, "I'm f*cked!"

After a long period of silence, he continued. "This is f*cked…I…I just gotta get out here." He grabbed his wallet and keys and headed for the door.

I might've given it 30 seconds before I realized I should stay close. I caught him about halfway down the block as he hurried to his car. "Yo, Jimmy – slow down, man, it's gonna be alright."

"No!" He turned to face me, his face red with anger. "THIS is a f*cking disaster! All of it. All of this is bullsh*t – it just keeps coming; it doesn't stop!"

His voice became quieter. "This is the worst thing that could've happened, and now, Jesus, I'm just not sure I want to go on anymore, not with all this bullsh*t."

He shook his head, looking down at the cement. "Not like this...I've had a good run."

"I can't do this anymore."

Jimmy had just been through a series of years you wouldn't wish on your worst enemy.

He awoke after 20-plus years to a loveless marriage and the sobering statement from his wife that she wanted a divorce. To their credit, they kept everything civil, to the point where their nearly adult children couldn't tell the difference (aside from their living arrangements).

Then, another breakup while on the rebound, coupled with what appeared to be the one bright spot on the horizon – a promising new business venture – which vanished before his eyes, never to see the light of day.

Jimmy was at the end of his rope.

I was concerned. I suspected it was crucial to keep the conversation going.

"I can't believe it," he continued walking again without looking back and marching at a hurried pace, flapping his arms around. "They f*cking screwed me! We had a deal! I just met with these f*ckers three days ago, and they were talking perks and health insurance, and...I don't know what the f*ck I'm gonna do...I have almost no money coming in now because I've dedicated the last three months to our f*cking business plan, the forecasting, and now...f*ck! I'm gonna be living out of my car!"

"Slow down," I pleaded. "Listen, please! That venture you were so excited about, these investors, the stock, the ownership – where did all that come from?"

I finally got him to face me. He just stared blankly.

"Where do you think '*it*' all came from, Jimmy?"

He gave me a confused, empty stare, but at least he was listening.

"Think about it!" I'm shouting at this point, trying to match his emotion and interrupt his train of thought.

I just wanted to do what I could to shift his perspective – to alter the narrative in his head.

"First," I pressed, "your girlfriend and that amazing opportunity you think was 'everything'? Where did *they* come from?"

Still blank.

"Damn it! Listen to me! You gotta find a way to keep your perspective here!"

Fortunately, I recalled that just a half year prior, a different business opportunity also vanished. An incredible contracting gig. Gone.

To Jimmy, though, it was a sign that all this sh*t just kept happening and would continue to happen. To me, it was proof there were more opportunities on their way.

It's important to point out that Jimmy isn't typically negative; he's usually one of the most upbeat, positive guys I know. To add to his great natural disposition is an off-the-chart intellect. But a long series of events, years in the making, beginning with his divorce, threw him way off-balance, skewing his perspective.

Recognizing Jimmy was fixated on the negatives, I did what I could to reassure him that I *knew* more great opportunities were on their way – it was just a matter of time.

The logic was simple; there were plenty of opportunities in his past, and there would be plenty more to come. The scene reminded me of the old tale Ronald Reagan loved to share about the twin boys:

> Worried their twin boys had developed very different personalities – one completely pessimistic, the other a total optimist, the parents sent them to see a psychiatrist.
>
> Attempting to shift the pessimist's outlook, the psychiatrist led him into a room full of toys. But instead of being elated, the boy began to cry. Confused, the psychiatrist asked, "Why are you so sad? You have all these toys you can play with!" The boy responds, "I'll probably just break them all!"
>
> Next, the psychiatrist, attempting to discourage the optimistic boy, led him to a room full of horse manure. Immediately elated, the boy climbed to the top of the pile and started to dig with his bare hands. Confused, the psychiatrist asked what he was doing. The boy responds enthusiastically, "With all this manure, there must be a pony in here somewhere!"

I persisted. "Jimmy, you do recall the prior opportunity just six months ago, right?"

"Yes, and that went to sh*t too! So what!?" he challenged me and was losing his patience.

"That's it! That's my point, brother! These opportunities are going to keep coming your way, I can assure you! It's not about the opportunities themselves, or even how they unfold, but how we *handle* them – how *we respond*!"

I deliberately used "we" to emphasize the idea that he wasn't alone. I wanted to remind him that WE ARE ALL tested, and the test isn't about the event or circumstance itself but instead how *we respond*.

I followed on that note. "Jimmy, how you respond, *right now*, to all this bullsh*t makes *all* the difference. It can either make you or break you."

"Be the bamboo baby," I urged. "Do *not* let this break you."

"Do NOT let this define you!"

Only a few years earlier, I had written *The Pressure Paradox*, so I had a well-stocked munitions galley. Among my many reference points was my own near bankruptcy as I tried to navigate our company through the great recession of 2008.

"Do not – I repeat, DO NOT let this define you. Hell, this could be a *blessing*!"

And with that statement, I surprised myself.

A new narrative and, with it, more possibilities entered the equation.

"Think about it this way these guys were already proving themselves to be dick-ish, right? Think about how many times you told me you thought they were already playing games in the negotiation."

"This might've been the best thing that could've happened to you! What if you got in deep, too quickly with these fools, and it became contentious, or worse, litigious?"

More possible storylines and hope emerged.

"You have another three months on your lease; stop with this, 'living out of my car' bullsh*t. Let's just slow down."

I reiterated the strategy. "The key here is to slow down and give this situation some time and space to process. A lot can happen in three months, trust me."

I'm certain that this is a universal experience. We fall into the illusion – the trap – of believing that we've reached the "end of our rope," and that we can see how the story ends (unfavorably). And I'm nearly certain everyone, at some point or another, experiences this.

John Lennon shared a brilliant observation about times like this: "Everything will be OK in the end, and if it isn't OK, it isn't the end."

Shifting our perspectives – imagining new and different possibilities and adding time and space to the horrific events that have thrown us off balance – is essential to moving forward constructively and envisioning new and different outcomes for our story.

It's worth noting that today (as of this writing), Jimmy is sharing his life with a wonderful woman and is doing some of the most creative and rewarding work he's ever accomplished. Further, it's astonishing to realize that *none* of his current success could have happened *unless* the above events took place.

Thus, *hope*, it turns out, is not optional.

Where there is hope in the future, there are possibilities in the present. Where there is hope in the future, there is happiness in the present.

People tend to say things like, "Hope isn't a strategy." Or, the classic Eleanor Roosevelt, "It takes as much energy to hope as it does to plan."

Eleanor is spot-on, *and* it isn't an either-or situation.

We should both plan *and* hope.

In fact, hope is bigger than any strategy. It would be tough to argue that hope isn't a prerequisite for any strategy.

Why would you play a game of chess (a purely strategic game) if you didn't have the hope that you could win? Regardless of the planning, preparation, and practice you might put in before a chess match, you'd still want to bring hope to the table.

You might chart (plan) a course to sail around the world. But there's never a captain – an adventurer – who didn't begin any journey without first packing hope.

Hope, therefore, is a prerequisite for any strategy: Hope is a disposition and a direction. Hope is the underlying thread of LIFE.

Where there is *life*, there is hope, and where there is hope, there is life.

I wrote about hope, opportunities, and even – incredibly – *STORY* when I wrote *The Pressure Paradox* in 2015, unknowingly foreshadowing this book:

***

[Excerpt: The Pressure Paradox]

Chances are excellent that the most successful people you know and admire have overcome pressure-riddled trials.

Right about now, you may be hearing a voice – a somber tone – telling you that your situation is somehow worse, different, and more challenging. It's the same voice that may even try to convince you that you aren't strong, good, smart, or skilled enough. Perhaps it's even a voice telling you that your goals are just too far out of reach. Why even bother?

In moments like these, it's important to recognize who is crafting *your* story.

Who is forecasting how it will end?

Where are you putting your attention, intention, and focus *most of the time*? (Recall the "Inner Circle" from the "Three Circles" earlier.)

You'd be hard-pressed to find a "situation" more challenging than that of Hellen Keller. And yet, she seemed to embody this idea of *positive refraction*. Somehow, she understood the importance of directing the pressure *optimistically*, assuring us:

"Optimism is the faith that leads to achievement. Nothing can be done without hope and confidence."

Where do that hope and confidence come from?

Who is writing your script?

[Then the kicker, I still don't recall writing in a book about pressure... some foreshadowing.]

Who knows for certain how your story will end?

***

Postscript:

As you might imagine, I wanted to ensure Jimmy was alright with me sharing this story. To his credit, appreciating its value and how it is very likely to provide hope and guidance for others, he obliged.

Jimmy did have one comment upon reflection several years removed from the chaotic events, and his insight is valuable.

Before I share it, it's important to notice how naturally – without any direction or guidance – his thoughts seamlessly flow into the following chapters of this book. Perfect serendipity, assuring us that the path we're following is correct.

Jimmy said, "I think my biggest 'sin' [interesting choice of words] was that I just didn't know *who* I was at that point in my life, and I didn't know *where* I was going."

"I was drifting, aimlessly."

Jimmy continued, "Everyone's occupation is sailor... we're either drifting without meaning and purpose, or we're headed toward an important destination."

A powerful observation seconded by the great Stoic Seneca, who remarked centuries ago: "If one does not know to which port one is sailing, no wind is favorable."

THE STORIES THAT
REALLY FREAKIN' MATTER

※

Michael Lewis

Author, *Money Ball*, *The Big Short*,
The Undoing Project and 50+ other works

As I've gotten older—I would say starting in my mid-to-late 20s—**I could not help but notice the effect on people of the stories they told about themselves**. If you listen to people, if you just sit and listen, you'll find that there are patterns in the way they talk about themselves.

There's the kind of person who is always the **victim** in any story that they tell. Always on the receiving end of some injustice. There's the person who's always kind of the **hero** of every story they tell. There's the smart person; they delivered the clever put-down...

There are lots of versions of this, and you've got to be very careful about **how you tell these stories because it starts to become you. You are—in the way you craft your narrative—kind of crafting your character**. And so, I did at some point decide, "*I am going to adopt self-consciously as my narrative, that I'm the happiest person anybody knows.*" And, it is amazing how happy-inducing it is.

24

139

"Chicks dig me because I rarely wear underwear, and when I do, it's usually something unusual. But now I know why I have always lost women to guys like you. I mean, it's not just the uniform. **It's the stories that you tell.** So much fun and imagination."
[points to the soldier next to him]
Stripes
~John Winger (Bill Murray)

"Your story is the greatest legacy that you will leave to your friends. It's the longest-lasting legacy you will leave to your heirs."
~*Steve Saint*

"I keep six honest serving men (they taught me all I knew). Their names are **What** and **Why** and **When** and **How** and **Where** and **Who**."

~ Rudyard Kipling

WHO?

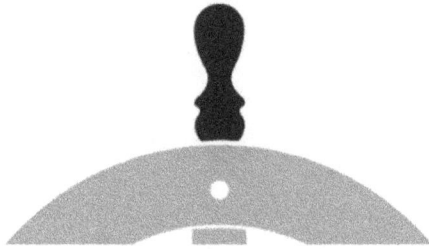

"The story that follows
'I am...' follows you."

The year was 1980. I was 11, and Bret, a new kid at our school, invited me to my first rock concert, The Who!

Even though it's been 30-plus years, the most memorable thing about Bret might've been his jet-black hair and light-blue eyes. I'm pretty sure the chicks dug him.

At the time, I knew nothing about the band The Who and recall very little about the concert other than I'd never seen so many people in one place. The event fueled my interest in rock-and-roll and the band. Their song, "Pinball Wizard," is still a favorite.

As the years went by, the experience morphed into a fair story and a bad pun. "You'll never guess *Who* I saw as my first concert?"

As I write this, it's nearly impossible to escape their signature song, "Who Are You?"

Lead singer Roger Daltrey implored, "Who are you? Who? Who? Who? Who?"

At its climax, Sir Daltrey takes the iconic song to the next level (in perfect harmony with this book, I might add) by dropping a good, old-fashioned F-bomb, belting out "Tell me WHO the F*ck are you!?" as the chorus chimes in, "are you…are you…are you…" and fades into the distance.

"Know thyself" is an Ancient Greek aphorism and the first of three Delphic maxims. It's followed by "nothing to excess" and "surety brings ruin." (A couple of tenets that could easily make for another book or two.)

Know thyself, in essence, promotes a keen self-awareness of one's strengths and weaknesses. As Zeno of Citium, founder of the Stoic school of philosophy, put it, "Nothing is more hostile to a firm grasp on knowledge than self-deception." Self-deception, on the other hand, simply equates to a lack of awareness.

Let's press pause for a moment and address the elephant in the room – the question that surfaces much like the Loch Ness monster on a cold, hazy morning in the Scottish Highlands.

If everything is a f*cking story, which stories are the most important? Which stories should we focus most of our attention on most of the time?

EVERYTHING Is A F*cking Story

If our lives are directed by our thoughts (most often taking the form of story), which are the seeds of our emotions and feelings (most of the time), influencing our decisions, actions, and behaviors (most of the time), all of which influence the skills and habits we develop over our lifetime, which stories have the most effect on our lives?

Which stories, at the end of the proverbial day, after you are long gone, and your story is written – will define your legacy?

Think about that. There will likely be thousands, if not hundreds of thousands, of stories developed over your lifetime.

You may be thinking, "How I'm remembered isn't really my problem," or, "How I'm remembered is out of my control." Or even, "The stories other people tell after I'm gone won't be my concern."

You may even be thinking along the lines of, "All I want to do is my best each day, be good to myself and others; my story will be whatever it will be."

Fair enough.

Yet, if you do good and are kind from one day to the next, your legacy (your story) will likely be that of a person who was kind and did well by others.

While this is an oversimplification, the core idea should not be lost: What we do from one day to the next – our actions, decisions, and behaviors (today) – reinforce the habits we form, contributing in large part to the person we become and the legacy we'll leave behind.

Thus, how you think now – even about your legacy story before your demise – can alter your present actions, decisions, and behaviors. This is the 3 Circles of Behavior Echo-System in effect.

<->Stories<->Habits<->Environment<->

To answer this all-important question, "Which stories are the most important?" we're going to take our cue from Kipling's brilliant poem (above) and begin at the very bottom. Let's start with "WHO?"

As in, "Who are you?"

Let's add Sir Daltrey's emphatic F-bomb to make the question reverberate in your head a bit longer and louder.

"Who the f*ck are you?"

Your answer to that all-important question is the *foremost* story that really freakin' matters.

In psychology, the term used to relate to oneself is often labeled the "self-concept," sometimes referred to as the "self-image," "self-identity," or maybe even "self-view" or "self-perspective." Whatever you want to call it, it's simply a collection of beliefs.

Correct. Stories.

Your self-concept can even be considered a mean or average of all the minute narratives or *scripts* you have about yourself and how you fit within the world at large.

Your self-concept and its related identity scripts are essentially a concoction of your past, present, and future experiences, beliefs, ideals, and values. It's a blend of all the scripts you've adopted – handed to you by others – and the ones you've created over a lifetime.

"I am a great driver." "I am not a good conversationalist." "I am a horrible singer." "I am a good swimmer." "I am bad at table tennis." "I am …."

In total, these scripts form your self-concept. While experts in behavioral sciences might disagree with this general definition or even what constitutes the self-concept, it is inarguable that our self-concept is made up; it's a *construct*.

The very phrase "self-concept" is rooted in the conceptual. Its etymology is "to collect, gather, or conceive." And the word conceptualize means "to form an idea of."

Thus, your self-concept originated from the same space as *everything else* – nothingness. It was derived from **nowhere**.

Further, these self-concept narratives tend to vary from one situation to the next, making them more like scripts – like those an actor reads – directing their thoughts, speech, decisions, and behaviors.

For whatever reason, it's rare for people to *conscientiously craft* a self-concept that aligns with their future goals and ideals. Instead, there tends to be little intentional guidance or planning.

In the next chapter, we highlight a historical great, a man who somehow recognized the power and importance of designing, with intention, a future self-concept – *WHAT* he desired to *become*. Fortunately for us, he documented his process and recounted with great alacrity its results after his 50-plus-years experiment.

In *The Habit Factor*, we revisit Aristotle's significant observation – the notion of "Tabula rasa" (blank slate) – which is the concept that *all* our knowledge comes from experience and perception. We arrive in this world with no beliefs, no values – we possess zero stories at birth.

You were born without a single "I am…" identity script. Recall the "Hypnotized" chapter and the golden awareness that, right now, we're all hypnotized to believe the stories that we've subscribed to, including our self-concept.

Ponder WHO you are right now and who you've become, and you're likely to realize that many, if not all, of your identity scripts are beliefs you hold.

Here's the interesting, albeit painful, revelation: You're likely carrying several (perhaps dozens) identity scripts that do not serve you, particularly as they relate to your goals and ideals.

That's worth reiterating: Many people continue to carry – in some cases, cling to – debilitating and non-serving stories and identity scripts that comprise their self-concept.

An obvious example comes from the "Worries" chapter within this book. Despite my writing efforts, perhaps hundreds of hours, I subconsciously retained an "I am no author" identity script.

The second crucial point: Your self-concept is – or should be – *evolving*, not static (for too long). Nothing remains static in the natural world, and trying to uphold a non-evolving self-concept goes against nature.

As we age, the world evolves. Technologies, medicines, science, and even knowledge changes. (Recall that we were once assured there were nine planets in our solar system.)

The world exists in a perpetual state of flux and transformation. Those who fail to keep learning, growing, evolving, and changing – those who carry a non-evolving self-concept – are ultimately left behind. Lao Tzu underscored the message this way: "When I let go of who I am, I become who I might be."

Eric Hoffer, the American moral and social philosopher, put it this way: "It's the learners who inherit the future. The learned usually find themselves equipped to live in a world that no longer exists." Then, there's all-time heavyweight champion Muhammad Ali, who said, "The man who views the world at 50 the same as he does at 20 has wasted 30 years of his life."

Many of us know *that* guy; let's call him Uncle Benny. Although, if you've seen the movie *Napoleon Dynamite*, his name is Uncle Rico. Good ol' Uncle Rico's life peaked as the quarterback of his high school football team.

Uncle Rico dreams, talks, and tells stories of his high school football days, even though they were 30-plus years ago.

By definition, a person with psychosclerosis doesn't evolve or adopt new *attitudes*, *opinions*, or *beliefs*. In short, a person suffering from psychosclerosis doesn't have too many *new stories about themselves*.

Like an oldies radio station, Uncle Rico plays the same sweet, familiar tunes (stories) over and over; they provide a sense of comfort and certainty. Only, it's a false sense of comfort – an illusion. The world has changed, yet Uncle Rico clings to a past identity – a petrified personality.

In 2006, Carol Dweck, a psychology professor at Stanford, published "Mindset," a study about implicit theories of intelligence. In short, her work underscored that the students who struggled the most tended to possess a "fixed" mentality or mindset. They were fixated upon a *static* belief (narrative) relative to their identity and capabilities.

These "fixed" mentality students did not possess what Dr. Dweck recognized as an essential trait for success: a "growth mindset." A growth mindset recognizes improvement in any endeavor as a *process* resulting from extended effort and practice over time. For purposes of our conversation here, we're going to tweak Dr. Dweck's label only slightly and call it a "growth identity or self-concept."

Consider your favorite actor. Think of a role they played exceptionally well, and you're likely to notice a simple truth: Their performance resulted from *intentional* and *deliberate practice*. This *practice* helped them to imbue the character deep into their subconscious.

Their award-winning performance was no accident. The actor cultivated the script and brought it to life – its lines, dialect, expressions, and mannerisms – all through practice.

They envisioned themself becoming the character, and they practiced both the envisioning and the supportive behaviors.

Undoubtedly, several readers are thinking, "This is garbage! If there's one thing I am not, it's a fake! I am and have always been the natural, real me. I am REAL!"

Well, my friend, I certainly fell into that line of thinking until the "reality" hit me: There is no "real" me, AND, of course, there *is* a real me.

The answer, once again, is BOTH!

The REAL me – my "real" identity – has been cultivated over a lifetime with consistency of behavior (habits) forging my character.

This is undoubtedly the "real" me, *and* it was something that emerged from nothing. It was *created!*

This awareness is worth repeating. The "WHO" in your "Who am I?" identity script can and should evolve and be revisited repeatedly.

If any script is found NOT to serve your present goals and ideals – not aiding you in your attempt to arrive there – it means it's time to edit, delete, or rewrite it.

Here's an example. One of my first major goals was an Ironman triathlon. The event begins with a 2.4-mile swim followed by a 112-mile bicycle ride and ends with a marathon, a 26.2-mile run. It was a big, hairy, stretch goal, to say the least. Yet, curiously, the first question I recall pondering was, *"Am I an Ironman?"* That is, can I envision myself completing an Ironman?

My answer: "I think so. It's possible. If others could do it, why not me? With commitment and the right training and practice, I believe I could become an Ironman."

Question time:

Are you _____? (artist, author, actor, comedian?)

Do you believe you can *become*_____?

How about saying it aloud: I am_____.

(Insert your goal and/or related identity in the blank.
How does it sound to you? How does it make you feel?
Remember, the actor practices their lines daily.)

This is an excellent starting point. By revisiting your "I
am…" identity script relative to your goals and ideals *before*
beginning, you might save yourself extended effort and
frustration. While this is not a requirement, it's highly
recommended.

This is where the psychological phenomenon "imposter
syndrome" tends to rear its ugly head. In short, imposter
syndrome is a pattern of belief reinforced by repetitive
thoughts and behaviors (habits) that prompts people to
ignore or even doubt their accomplishments and
achievements. Instead, they cling to a former, more
comfortable self-identity. They become (unconsciously)
confused by their work, changes, and growth and are even
fearful they'll be revealed as a "fraud."

Sound familiar?

Recall the prior "Worries" chapter.

"Human psyches are complicated and messy things,"
says Todd Herman, bestselling author and high-
performance coach. In Herman's coaching practice, they
teach a technique known as identity assimilation. This is the
identification and rapid adaptation of an alter ego.

In his bestseller, *The Alter Ego Effect*, Herman posits that
the quickest way for many people to be more effective and
perform better is to simply assume an "alter ego."[25]

Rather than trying to reprogram (hypnotize) oneself into a new self-concept, which could take months or years, one can rapidly switch to a new "I am" identity as quickly as changing clothes.

By slipping into a new identity, similar to Superman throwing on his cape and tights, you *feel* and *act* differently – optimally, for a performance that awaits.

Herman's work points to many greats, particularly athletes, who "step into" often superhero-like alter egos before, even during athletic performances.

Herman shares his own transformation by recounting that it took wearing glasses for him to feel smarter. "Eventually, that happened to me [referring to a Cary Grant statement about pretending to be someone and then *becoming* that person]. At first, I'd put the glasses on and call myself Richard until, at some point, I didn't need the name or the glasses to feel smart or respected or confident. I just was. I just started showing up that way…it became a *habit*."

This is more proof that our habits build our character, affecting our sense of identity. Importantly, our character and identity influence our behaviors and habits. The influence of each underscores the "echo" in the Behavior Echo-System.

Regardless of the method – rapid assimilation or slow growth of habits and skills – the lesson remains the same: The requirement to address a former self-identity is fundamental to performance and character, which is crafted by our habits.

Have you ever heard the phrase, "What would Jesus do?" (Insert any character or admired person.) This is a clear example of how your behavior, actions, and decisions can be driven by an associated *character* or *identity*.

By approaching this behavior model (Three Circles) with awareness, anyone can more easily let go of a former self-identity and assume a new one, one that supports their current goals and ideals.

Further, this behavior model demonstrates why and how conditions like Imposter Syndrome exist. Clinging to a former, comfortable self-concept often drives incongruent behaviors relative to new aspirations.

Thus, a new self-concept – a new self-identity ("Who I am" script) can absolutely be both assimilated quickly and cultivated over time with practice.

Now, to be clear, if you don't possess the basic capabilities or have the existing skills and habits (middle circle), affirmations alone will not be sufficient. This is where many self-help Goo-Roos' messaging misses the mark; they tend to focus upon just one core influencer.

A more holistic approach to goal achievement and personal transformation addresses all significant influencers.

<<Story>><<Skills/Habits>><<Environment>>

Before you can convince others of any new identity, it's helpful to convince yourself first. Intentionally cultivating the requisite skills and habits (middle circle) helps to forge the new identity narrative and make it "real."

The question arises: What about all the people who are effective yet never practice new identity scripts or conscientiously work on their self-concept?

Whether done consciously or not, they have worked on them. Much like habit formation, self-concepts and identity scripts are constantly being formed, often without conscientious thought. Consider how people form bad habits all the time without planning. The same is true for identity scripts and self-concepts. The message here is that, with awareness, this work can be done conscientiously.

After teaching and studying habits for nearly two decades, this simple statement may be helpful: Good habits happen when planned; bad habits happen on their own.

The same can be said for your self-concept and "I AM…" identity scripts.

For most, self-concepts form naturally without much intention or creativity. Over our lifetime, we just adopt them; they appear real, true, and accurate.[25]

As recounted in the "Worries" chapter, I find myself wishing I'd understood this notion better. If I had, I could have started with my "I AM…" script before I'd written a single word of *The 3 C's of SuCCCess*.

"Can you envision yourself as an author?" I should have asked myself.

Yes or no.

Do not pass Go.

Garbage In. Garbage Out. **Greatness In. Greatness Out.**

If you have goals and ideals that will require you to become a different person and forge a new character – and my experience tells me that those are the very best goals to

---

[25] Recall Michael Lewis's conscientious adoption of his character from the opening quotation.

have – then checking your "I am identity script" at the door is the first key to unlocking it.

Jim Rohn, the late, great motivational speaker, put it this way: **"You should set a goal big enough that in the process of achieving it, you become someone worth becoming."** (*emphasis me.*)

One might argue that the formation of any new habits and skills will almost certainly drive a new self-concept and "I AM..." identity scripts.

My experience tells me that is accurate, *and* it tends to be a much slower process. There is no reason one can't work on *both* – the self-concept and supportive habits. Arguably, this is precisely what effective people do naturally without conscientious effort. They jointly cultivate their identity script (Inner Circle/*Story*) and develop new habits and skills (Middle Circle) at the same time.

By cultivating the requisite skills and habits *and* possessing a supportive identity script (imaginative narrative), all within a conducive environment, anyone can reinvent themselves.

After all, this is precisely what facilitates the successful rehabilitation of prisoners – a reimagining of their self-concept, one that is consistent with rehabilitation.

Their new identity story/script might sound like: "I am a law-abiding citizen." "I am no longer a criminal." "I am *not* the kind of person who steals."

A consistent theme among prisoners who avoid recidivism is that they see themselves with a new self-concept; they possess new identity scripts.[26]

155

EVERYTHING Is A F*cking Story

Someone may say, "Well, any rehabilitation of prisoners involves far more than just a new self-concept. They almost certainly had some counseling and additional support once released from prison. They probably also had a safe place to live and maybe even a job to help them rehabilitate."

Such a statement only affirms the **3 Circles of Behavior Echo-System** and how *all* the component "circles" must be involved in the *transformation process.*

Inner Circle <->Identity Story & Scripts

Middle Circle <-> Behaviors, Skills, and Habits

Outer Circle <-> Environment

Personal transformation is metamorphosis.

All metamorphosis, by definition, demands a change in habits. The butterfly possesses entirely different habits than the caterpillar.

What does your desired transformation look like?

What sort of self-concept and corresponding identity scripts (story) must you possess to enable your desired transformation as you move toward your most important goals and ideals?

Let's begin here:

WHO are you?

"I AM..."

WHAT?

*"The only person you are destined to
become is the person you decide to become."
~Ralph Waldo Emerson*

The year was 1726, and a 20-year-old Benjamin Franklin
set sail toward Philadelphia. It was a return voyage on the
Berkshire, leaving London after two semi-difficult and
confusing years as a journeyman and printer apprentice. He
wrote in his autobiography, "I was grown tired of London,
remembered with pleasure the happy months I had spent in
Pennsylvania, and wished again to see it."

As recounted in Walter Isaacson's brilliant biography,
Benjamin Franklin: An American Life,[27] Franklin was

157

determined to *become better* after accumulating significant debt and encountering a few disappointing business arrangements.

Ben felt he could benefit from improving his character, an astonishing observation at such a young age. His reflection was undoubtedly aided by a transatlantic journey extended by weeks due to unfavorable winds.

If we were a seagull perched high up on the schooner's mast, we might've witnessed a young Ben standing on the deck, looking out over the horizon, peering into his future, both literally and figuratively, asking one simple, life-altering question: **"What do I want to become?"**

In his autobiography, nearly 55 years later, Dr. Franklin seemed somewhat mystified by his younger self:[28]

> We sail'd from Gravesend on the 23rd of July, 1726. For the incidents of the voyage, I refer you to my Journal, where you will find them all minutely related. *Perhaps the most important part of that journal is THE PLAN [50] to be found in it, which I formed at sea, for regulating my future conduct in life. It is the more remarkable, as being formed when I was so young, and yet being pretty faithfully adhered to quite thro' to old age.*

At just 20, Ben took significant time to pause and reflect, removing himself from his present-day worries and challenges to ask, "What do I want to become?"

More powerful still, his plan – "THE PLAN," as he called it, "for moral perfection" – held the process for how he would get there.

As part of his scheme, Ben identified 12 traits (virtues) that he believed he should cultivate. When refined, these virtues would help to create his ideal future character.

As recounted in *The Habit Factor*, Aristotle taught that the path to virtue is via habit. For instance, if you have the habit of being honest, you'll be known to possess the virtue of honesty. A person with the habit of being frugal will be known to possess the virtue of frugality.

Virtues are an established order of behavior that can be intentionally crafted through mindful, conscientious practice.

As a quick aside: The intentional cultivation of habits helps us reach our goals *and* aids in the formation of our character. This is one of the most critical lessons I learned and now teach when it comes to habit development.

Habit is a means toward two ends.

1) **Character**: Who we become.
2) **Achievements and Accomplishments**: What we accomplish in our lifetime.

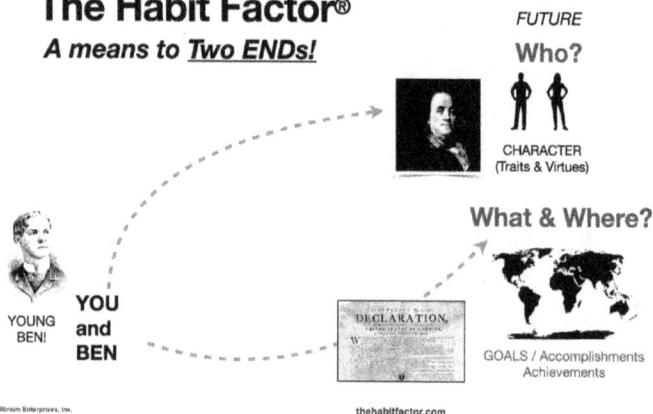

The Habit Factor®
A means to _Two ENDs!_

FUTURE
Who?

CHARACTER
(Traits & Virtues)

What & Where?

YOUNG
BEN!

**YOU
and
BEN**

DECLARATION

GOALS / Accomplishments
Achievements

© Equilibrium Enterprises, Inc.

thehabitfactor.com

Image ©2020 Equilibrium Enterprises: Automatic Goals

I sensed that when it came to human habit development, there was more to cultivating habits than the established science, which emphasized (a bit too much for my taste) "The Habit Loop" and Cue Routine Reward (derived from studying rodents).

The more I reflected upon habit, the more clearly I saw that the act of planning – using our human capacities of choice, intention, and reflection – is how we can intentionally cultivate habits that serve our goals.

The truth is that habits, mostly bad habits, are often created _without_ any plan. It's the good, valuable habits that tend to require intentional thought – _a plan_.

As a rule of thumb:

Good habits happen when planned; bad habits happen on their own.

Thus, The Habit Factor's methodology, P.A.R.R. (Plan, Act, Record, & Reassess), affirms the innate human capacities of **Choice, Intention,** and **Reflection.** These elements help to account for The Habit Factor's efficacy.[26]

We can rest assured that our buddy Ben had no preconceptions about Cue, Routine, Reward, or "The Habit Loop." Instead, he intentionally set out to cultivate habits via his own tracking process, which ultimately produced many of the virtues he sought.

His precepts are detailed below (copied straight from his autobiography):

These names of virtues, with their precepts, were:
1. Temperance
Eat not to dullness; drink not to elevation.

2. Silence.
Speak not but what may benefit others or yourself; avoid trifling conversation.

3. Order.
Let all your things have their places; let each part of your business have its time.

---

[26] Nearly every *current* study of habit formation with humans involves planning and recording – choice, intention, and reflection.

4. Resolution.
Resolve to perform what you ought; perform without fail
what you resolve.

5. Frugality.
Make no expense but to do good to others or yourself; i.e.,
waste nothing.

6. Industry.
Lose no time; be always employ'd in something useful; cut
off all unnecessary actions.

7. Sincerity.
Use no hurtful deceit; think innocently and justly; and, if
you speak, speak accordingly.

8. Justice.
Wrong none by doing injuries or omitting the benefits that
are your duty.

9. Moderation.
Avoid extremes; forbear resenting injuries so much as you
think they deserve.

10. Cleanliness.
Tolerate no uncleanliness in body, clothes, or habitation.

11. Tranquility.
Be not disturbed at trifles, or at accidents common or
unavoidable.

12. Chastity.

13. Humility.
Imitate Jesus and Socrates.

You'll notice that there are 13 virtues, not the 12 Ben
initially mentioned.

Well, it turns out Ben has a cute little story about his 13th virtue, **humility**. A Quaker friend suggested that Ben could stand to benefit from some added humility. To his credit, Ben took the recommendation in stride, writing:

> My list of virtues contain'd at first but twelve; but a Quaker friend having kindly informed me that I was generally thought proud; that my pride show'd itself frequently in conversation; that I was not content with being in the right when discussing any point, but was overbearing, and rather insolent, of which he convinc'd me by mentioning several instances; I determined endeavouring to cure myself, if I could, of this vice or folly among the rest, and I added **Humility** to my list, giving an extensive meaning to the word.

> I cannot boast of much success in acquiring the *reality* of this virtue, but I had a good deal with regard to the appearance of it. I made it a rule to forbear all direct contradiction to the sentiments of others, and all positive assertion of my own... I adopted, instead, "I conceive," "I apprehend," or "I imagine a thing to be so or so; or it so appears to me at present."

> When another asserted something that I thought an error, I deny'd myself the pleasure of contradicting him abruptly, and of showing immediately some absurdity in his proposition; and in answering I began by observing that in certain cases or circumstances his opinion would be right, but in the present case there appear'd or seem'd to me some difference, etc.

I soon found the advantage of this change in my manner; the conversations I engag'd in went on more pleasantly. The modest way in which I propos'd my opinions procur'd them a readier reception and less contradiction; I had less mortification when I was found to be in the wrong, and I more easily prevail'd with others to give up their mistakes and join with me when I happened to be in the right.

The wisdom in Ben's reflection denotes the remarkable value he gained from his *practice* of tracking habits to form his virtues. It may even be priceless for anyone, like me, who has found their pride and opinions to be a bit (or a lot) off-putting.

Ben's observation seconds one of my favorite Thomas Jefferson quotes, "Always take things by their smooth handle."

To Ben's surprise, even the virtue of humility was enhanced, although he confessed, "…I never arrived at the perfection I had been so ambitious of obtaining, but fell far short of it, yet **I was, by the endeavour, a better and a happier man than I otherwise should have been if I had not attempted it.**"

So, *WHAT* is it that you want to *BEcome*?

It doesn't matter if you're 18 or 68.

Everything is in a process of perpetual becoming. The question is, **"What are you becoming?"**

Your ideal future awaits, and it only arrives one single day at a time; those are the rules for everyone. No one's ideal future can arrive any faster.

Thus, knowing WHERE (next chapter) you are headed (*sailing to*) – in what direction your ideal future lies – is the first key to arriving.

What challenges excite you?

What goals or ideals inspire you?

What personal, communal, or world problems motivate, anger, frustrate, or energize you?

Abraham Maslow put it this way: "What a man can be, he must be." Maslow described this as "self-actualization" – the pursuit of one's full potential. Their ideal self is a requirement for a fulfilled and happy life.

When you consider the people who seem fulfilled and happy (most of the time), content with their life and contributions (for the most part), they seem to fall into this category of "self-actualizing" individuals.

Further, self-actualization tends to lead to massive creative breakthroughs and accomplishments – whether it's the incandescent lightbulb, personal computer, electric vehicles, or the theory of relativity. These types of breakthroughs are possible because basic needs have been addressed. (See Maslow's hierarchy of needs below.)

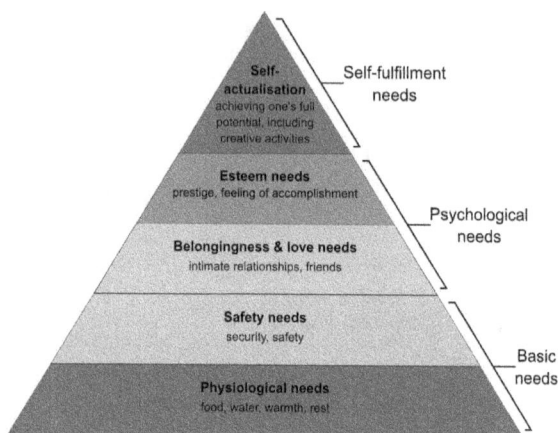

Maslow's Hierarchy of Needs, Wikipedia[29]

There's a good chance that your current frustration, anger, and feeling of being "stuck" means that while your basic needs are met, you're without a creative pursuit to foster self-actualization.

The good news is that once you recognize and understand this challenge, you can see it for what it is: a challenge for you to step on the path and heed your call.

Maslow writes, "A musician must make music, an artist must paint, a poet must write, if he is to be ultimately at peace with himself. What a man can be, he must be. This need we may call self-actualization. . .This tendency might be phrased as the desire to become more and more what one is, to become everything that one is capable of becoming."

Here, again, we notice a fundamental truth:

Intelligence is goal-directed behavior.

In life, *goals are not optional.*

What are your goals?

What must you become?
* (assuming you have food/water, shelter, job, safety)

Brian Tracy likes to say, "If you were woken out of a cold sleep at 3 a.m., you should be able to recount your top three goals instantly." Now, that presumes, of course, that your basic needs are met. For instance, if the first two levels of needs are not met, chances are very good you're not reading this book.

However, for most people, if your basic needs are met, but you're not answering "The Call," you'll likely remain frustrated, confused, perhaps even angry, and you may not even know why.

Since everything is in a constant state of change, we have (assuming our basic needs are addressed) the opportunity to drive, direct, and influence the changes we'd like to see in our lives, as much as – and perhaps more than – the changes our environment imposes on us.

This is the sentiment behind Peter Drucker's famous statement: "The best way to predict the future is to create it." Another corollary: The best way to navigate the bend in the road is to be the person bending it.

What goal or ideal are your intuition and intelligence guiding you toward? (More on this later.)

What is your great quest?

Reflect deeply upon the "Meaning" chapter and Joseph Campbell's Hero's Journey. You are the Hero. Your quest is standing right before you. Are you denying "The Call" or leaning into it?

Will it be easy? Unlikely. Will it get easier over time? Most certainly.

Oprah Winfrey put it this way:

"The biggest adventure you can take is to live the life of your dreams."

Live the life of *your* dreams.

Oprah undoubtedly had more disadvantages and hurdles than most. Today, she's a billionaire. My guess, though, is the positive impact she's had on millions of people's lives is far more significant to her. She's been a shining example, inspiring others to push onward and do their best with what they have, one day at a time.

That is the only way anyone realizes "success."

Success isn't "out there." Success is found within, created and experienced one day at a time.

WHERE?

*"The great thing in this world is not so much
where we stand, as in what direction we are moving
— we must sail sometimes with the wind and
sometimes against it — but we must sail, and not
drift, nor lie at anchor."*
~ *Oliver Wendell Holmes*

Thud.

Ol' Ollie just dropped the mic!

If intelligence is goal-directed behavior, any human who deems themself intelligent must set sail. They cannot lie at anchor for too long.

Drifting for too long is resignation; it's the abdication of control. It means you've let go of the steering wheel.

Drifting for too long becomes a habit – an illness, even – rooted in fear and worry.

Drifting for too long is what pieces of wood, garbage, and dead fish do, washing up on a desolate beach along with all the other flotsam and jetsam.

Bad things happen when one drifts for too long.

As covered in the Preface, life is a delicate balance. Some might even call it a dance between two supernatural forces – the things we can control and the things we cannot.

We can't always choose which ocean we find ourselves in, but we can choose *where* we want to go and how we set our sails.

By directing our stories with intention and harnessing the wind, we can direct and influence where we want to go.

While it's a certainty that storms will blow us off course (events beyond our control) and we will be forced to lie at anchor, once the storm passes, we must set sail.

No storm lasts forever.

It's understandably romantic to think, "Not all who wander are lost," recalling J.R.R. Tolkien's famous passage. Yet, those who cite it are missing the point, not to mention the accompanying lines: "Not all who wander are lost; the old that is strong does not wither, deep roots are not reached by the frost."

Strength and deep roots only come from *purpose* – a sense of direction. Strength and deep roots are nature's way of helping us survive storms.

The sad truth is that most who wander for too long *are lost*.

Thus, the third of the six most critical f*cking stories that really matter is:

Where the f*ck are you sailing?

Where do you want to go?

Not just physically but mentally, emotionally, spiritually, socially, and professionally,

That's correct: "Sailing" to new and beautiful destinations happens on multiple levels or dimensions. Zig Ziglar used to say, "Aim at nothing, and you'll hit it every time!"

Humans operate on several distinct, extraordinary, and *interconnected* dimensions. Collectively, they culminate in our well-being and peace of mind.

Peace of mind, arguably the ultimate destination, is also, paradoxically, a *starting* point. Peace of mind is the pot of gold at *both* ends of the rainbow; it's a blend of *all* the core human dimensions.

Financial success without peace of mind is relatively worthless. Professional success without peace of mind is arguably meaningless. Any "success" without peace of mind is shallow and short-lived.

Peace of mind is a unique balance of grit mixed with acceptance. It is determination beautifully blended with adaptability and surrender.

Peace of mind is a choice as much as a consequence; it's the harmony that arises when our actions and behaviors are aligned – in complete congruence – with our values. This underscores N. R. Narayana Murthy's observation, "A clear conscience is the softest pillow."

Peace of mind is the fence around worthwhile success.

The core four dimensions – the primary factors that constitute wellness and peace of mind – are Mind, Body, Social, and Spiritual (in no particular order). The next four are Emotional, Professional, Financial, and Adventure/Lifestyle.

Peace of mind is knowing that you are absolutely perfect *and* that you could use some work.

In short: Peace of mind comes from embracing paradox – becoming a *contented achiever*.

As Angela Duckworth wrote in her wonderful book, *Grit*:[30]

> Why were the highly accomplished so dogged in their pursuits? For the most, there was no realistic expectation of ever catching up to their ambitions. In their own eyes they were never good enough. They were the opposite of complacent. And yet, in a very real sense, they were satisfied, being unsatisfied.

The concept of being satisfied *and* unsatisfied simultaneously is the antithesis of dichotomous thinking, often the cause of much disharmony.

Appreciating wholeness fosters the ability to hold two opposing ideas and, at the very least, the ability to appreciate each.

Can you be satisfied and dissatisfied?

Can you be content and discontent?

Can you be attached and detached?

Peace of mind is found by embracing paradox *and* assuming control of the helm – your life's steering wheel – directing the stories you tell yourself about yourself and your world.

You *can* control your thoughts (most of the time); you *can* direct your stories – the ones that drive your feelings and emotions (most of the time).

Your thinking (stories) directs your attention and *where* your vessel is headed. This brings to mind William Blake's quote, "We become what we behold."

Recall Jimmy's story from the "Hope" chapter. Notice how he unwittingly said, "Everyone's occupation is sailor." Everyone is traveling somewhere; everyone is on a journey. Given the theme of this book, it's a treasure of an observation.

You are a sailor.

Jimmy recounted this insight only after extended periods of reflection. Once again, Jimmy's statement:

"I was drifting, aimlessly… we're either drifting without meaning and purpose, or we're headed toward an important destination."

The beauty is that once we identify a destination (**where**), the other dimensions are almost always dragged along for the ride.

How do you know *where* to head? How do you know where you should direct your time and attention? Often the first, best place is *into* the wind. Even an anchored sailboat directs itself into the wind. Chances are good there is resistance (wind) in your life right now – problems, challenges, and pressure. Ignoring challenges often helps problems fester.

Similarly, leaning into your goals and ideals helps you direct and create the changes you want to see in your life.

The result? Personal growth, knowledge, experience, and wisdom, supporting Zig Ziglar's observation: "You'll want to set a goal so big that you cannot achieve it until you grow into the person who can."

That is precisely what goal achievement and personal transformation represent: **a process of becoming.**

To become something new and different, to experience a personal transformation, is a process of metamorphosis – the assumption of new and different habits.

You either intentionally direct the change, or the change directs you. As covered previously, the truth is that it's *both*. Jim Rohn told people: "The good news is you are going to arrive in 10 years! The question is, *where?*"

When it comes to intentional transformation and pursuing your goals, it's essential to realize that your *existing* habits will act as a shackle; they will be tough to break. The first step in changing any habit pattern is to become aware. You'll need to mentally step outside the 3 Circles of Behavior Echo-System and notice *where* the stories (mindset), behaviors (habits), feelings and emotions, and environment have taken you today.

What new habit-driven patterns of behavior and thought will be required to get to *where* you want to go tomorrow?

Will you need to adjust your mindset and story? Will you need to adjust your *Who* and *What* scripts?

Will you need to modify your environment?[27]

Typically, the answer is yes to all the above.

Once we recognize *where* we want to go compared to *where* we are, it's crucial to lean on the HERO's story checklist.

Here's an example of what changes can occur when we adopt a HERO's mindset:

Broken Story:
I'm never going to make it. We're so far in this hole, and now, at my age (58), I should have an established career and, at the very least, my own house. I'm so pissed off at my boss and spouse and the whole goddamn planet for not understanding what was supposed to happen. This is not the life I was looking for!

Working Story:
I am responsible for where I am now. The fact is, people change careers all the time, even at my age. There's been a lot of good to come from my "situation," and I can

---

[27] More in the "Application" section.

see that by putting in the time and energy to establish new thought and behavior patterns, I can create the new, positive changes I want to see in the future. Garbage In. Garbage Out. Greatness In. Greatness Out. I know I can turn my results around. It begins with *me.*

Which story is *hopeful, empowering, responsible,* and *optimistic?*

Is it possible to reach a goal without a HERO's mindset? Maybe. Rest assured, it will be far more challenging, and I've yet to come across an example where a doubtful, fearful, non-hopeful story proves effective.

In every class I teach on "Profound Transformation" or goal achievement, a consistent set of mindset characteristics (story scripts) emerges *regardless* of the goal or desired transformation. It doesn't matter if the goal is to become a piano player or a kite-surfer or if you want to lose 35 pounds, be a better spouse, or attain the CEO position of a company.

While the HERO's script may seem a bit cheesy, it's a simple way to ensure that your personal narratives are facilitating your efforts and not opposing them.

The HERO's script is a starting point to ensure that our efforts are backed by congruent thought patterns conducive to the transformation and desired goal.

Here's the HERO's script framework:
- ☑ Hopeful
- ☑ Empowered
- ☑ Responsible
- ☑ Optimistic

Is your story Hopeful?

Can you envision a successful path forward to affect and realize the desired transformation, ideal or goal?

Are you Empowered?

Do you believe you can gain the necessary information, tools, and resources (including people) to affect the change? An empowered I AM script sounds like: "I AM capable" and "I AM confident."

Are you Responsible for changing your story?

If not you, who is going to make this change happen? Who can do your pushups for you?

Finally, is your story Optimistic?

Despite the innumerable setbacks you have faced thus far and will undoubtedly face going forward, can you stay optimistic, most of the time? Can you appreciate that each setback is moving you closer to a more favorable outcome, even if you can't quite see it yet?

The HERO's script is a framework and checklist that affirms that the minimum viable mindset traits are intact. While the acronym may seem like child's play, it's powerful and helps ensure your mindset *facilitates* where you are trying to go.

Here's the next essential consideration regarding the idea of Where? Arguably, this might be your first consideration:

From where are you sailing?

In other words, where are you emotionally anchored right now?

It's important to realize that your where is not just a physical location; it's also an emotional disposition. Consider your emotional starting point most of the time.

Just as every sailboat has a homeport, every person has an emotional homeport – a default disposition. Tony Robbins practically screams this sentiment: "Everyone has an emotional home!"

Where (emotionally) is your vessel docked most of the time?

Before any journey begins, a sailor must know from where they are departing. Unfortunately, many never take the time to really understand their emotional homeport – their default disposition most of the time.

We all know people who experience extremely tough circumstances, events, tragedies, and accidents yet maintain an emotional starting point of **hope**.

Recall Klyn Elsbury (from the "Meaning" chapter). She was born with cystic fibrosis at birth (a life sentence) and given a life expectancy of *maybe* 14 years. Somehow, despite this terrible prognosis and spending nearly 40% of her waking days in the hospital, she still finds hope and approaches life (more days than not) with a HERO's mindset!

It's a bit trendy to discount hope; many Goo-Roos do. While we've already devoted an entire chapter to the topic, it's worth sharing a quick story.

While teaching "Success Skills" for Junior Achievement in the early 2000s, I posed a semi-tough question to my high school class: "What is the opposite of success?"

Several students called out, "Failure!"

Yet, we realized something as we analyzed and discussed many of history's greats, including Henry Ford, Walt Disney, Amelia Earhart, Abraham Lincoln, and Thomas Edison. (Today's list might've included Sara Blakely, Steve Jobs, Elon Musk, Jeff Bezos, etc.)

It turns out that "failure" is anything but the opposite of success. In fact, it's really a prerequisite. Thomas Edison, for instance, only succeeded with the incandescent lightbulb after reportedly thousands of "failures." Thousands.

Thus, collectively stumped (myself included), we silently contemplated the opposite of success.

Minutes ticked by. Then, a young lady in the front of the room threw up her hand with great confidence.

"Hopelessness!" she shouted.

My knees buckled a bit. My back fell up against the whiteboard. I clapped and yelled, "Wow! Thank you! That's fantastic!"

It was a brilliant hypothesis.

Without hope, there is little or no life. Without hope, there is little or no energy to press on. Without hope (as my good buddy Mitch W. Steel wrote in the 3C's of SuCCCess), nobody can possibly realize their ideal future.

Hope provides everyone an equal footing and a fighting chance. Hope never arrives without bringing its cousin opportunity.

To be hopeless, unfortunately, only assures failure.

We can rest assured that our heroes begin from a default disposition – an emotional homeport – of *hope* (more days than not).

Chances are good that you can quickly identify a handful of people in your life (perhaps people you know intimately well) who begin each day from the opposite homeport, one of **hopelessness and even despair.**

They see whatever situation that befalls them as a tragedy, something happening *to* them rather than *for* them. They have little hope – in some cases, no hope – and that is a dangerous place to have your vessel docked most of the time.

There's never been a statue or a public memorial erected to honor the cynic, the *hopeless*, or the pessimist.

Those whom we admire likely start from a default predisposition toward hope. Think about community leaders, adventurers, athletes, scientists, inventors, entrepreneurs, and everyday heroes like parents and teachers working hard to ensure a better future for children.

Further, these people have likely developed the habit of *responding* to challenges instead of reacting, most of the time.

Responding – taking the time to pause, reflect and consider the consequences of one's actions rather than reacting–affirms one's hopeful disposition.

Recall Shay Eskew from the "Meaning" chapter. To quickly recap, Shay was the victim of severe childhood burns due to an accident.

If you're wondering what a HERO's default disposition should be and what responding to adversity looks or sounds like, here's a quick sample:

(The following excerpt was cut and pasted from Shay's Facebook post of 1/11/21 with permission).

> Operation rebuild has begun. This is us (selfie above) on our way to Tampa for the surgery scheduled for Tues morning. I anticipate being in the hospital 1-2 weeks. I've kept this on the down low for several months as I didn't want it to detract from the holidays and everything we had planned. I'd rather live for the moment and tackle life's challenges as they come.
>
> In short, I'm having a skin flap taken from my back (left lat) and inserted into my neck. Basically they'll harvest a section of skin with its own blood supply and graft the skin and blood vessels into my neck. Not sure how big the flap will be as it will depend once they release the scar tissue. If successful, this will reduce the scar tissue contractures on my neck and face that over the last 10 years have progressed to become unbearable. I won't bore you with the details only to say it's chronic pain 24hr a day that only feels better with exercise. Endorphins are great medicine.

People have asked what is the recovery. Honestly I don't know and would rather not know to prevent me from postponing or waiting for the "perfect time." It's also better not knowing so loved ones don't worry. It will be fine no matter what happens and there's no sense wasting energy worrying about things outside of your control. The way I approach surgery is to just do what you know needs to be done, endure whatever comes your way and commit to never quitting to attain the life you want. Embrace the suck! Super thankful to the amazing team at Sons of the Flag for making this surgery a reality... Let's do this!!!!

This is an example of a very enviable emotional homeport. Can we all be this brave in the face of such uncertainty? Not likely.

If one's emotional homeport (disposition) exists on a spectrum of 1-10, Shay's is over on the high end, the 10-ish realm, relative to his bravery, courage, and hope.

Shay's HERO Score is as close to 10 as it gets.

What's your HERO score?
Where is your emotional default disposition?

Now let's travel to the other end of the spectrum, where we'll find the "others." Think about people who collapse at the slightest inconvenience: the wrong drink is served, their flight is delayed, the Wi-Fi on the plane is out of order, or the weather sucks. When their expectations are vanquished and plans are disrupted, they go BERSERK!

These are the emotionally fragile and the easily triggered; their HERO score is around 1. They *react* far more often than they *respond*. And, when they react, it's typically aggressive, sometimes even combative, fed by a bizarre sense of entitlement.

There are so many emotionally charged and fragile souls that their outbursts have been caught on social media and they've been given names.

They're so quick to pounce and complain. They blame and shame others and point fingers, even playing the victim card at every opportunity.

So, what's the source of such emotional fragility?

It's simply the emotionally charged stories they carry around in their gunnysack. While any one of these stories individually may be barely noticeable, each adds weight to the burden.

Imagine that I've handed you one four-pound brick. Just four pounds, fairly light. Now, hold it over your head for a minute. That would be easy to do, right?

What happens if I ask you to hold that same "light" four-pound brick over your head for six hours? Could you do it? It's just the same four pounds.

Chances are excellent that you could not do it. The physical and emotional toll – the energy required – would be exhausting. Similarly, carrying emotionally draining stories around for weeks, months, years – even decades – becomes unsustainable. Something has to give.

Then, these people wonder why they can't seem to get any closer to their most important goals.

Recall the psychological term "gunnysacking" from previous chapters, and it's easy to see how these emotionally charged stories help to validate someone's poor reactions and emotional disposition.

If we're all sailors (as Jimmy put it), in theory, we're all traveling somewhere. We're on a journey toward our future, hopefully, an ideal future.

Our emotional homeport matters because our quest is either made easier or more challenging based upon where we begin our journey.

Winston Churchill said it like this: "You'll never reach your destination if you stop and throw stones at every dog that barks."

Every journey requires energy; all goal achievement demands energy. Energy is the price you pay *daily* to move toward your ideal future – your great QUEST.

Your energy is limited!

Ralph Waldo Emerson echoed the sentiment, "The price of *anything* is the amount of *life* you exchange for it."

Therefore, to complete any quest, attain any goal, and achieve any personal transformation, energy is expended either efficiently or inefficiently.

Habits are the most efficient use of behavior energy.

While good habits are difficult to develop at first, they yield magnificent rewards later.

Thus, one of the best investments you can make today, with your limited energy, is to begin developing the core, supportive habits required for your future goals and ideals.

How well you manage your behavior and emotional energy (*disposition*) today will massively impact *where* you'll end up in the future.

WHY?

"Tiger got to hunt, bird got to fly;
Man got to sit and wonder 'why, why, why?'
Tiger got to sleep, bird got to land;
Man got to tell himself he understand."
~ Kurt Vonnegut, Cat's Cradle

Logic.
Order.
Reason.
Our psychological well-being is often based on our
ability to understand "things." This understanding is rooted
in reason, which is cultivated – even curated – to provide a

sense of safety and security within ourselves and our surroundings.

Despite the inexplicable phenomena around us, we (humans) perpetually fool ourselves into a sense of "knowing." Singer and songwriter Jack Johnson put it brilliantly: "We're clever, but we're clueless."

We can send people into space and instantly beam information from one corner of the world to the other, but we can't explain the most basic of phenomena, such as why a heart begins to beat or even why humans exist.

So, we conveniently explain *everything* with a story, one that provides some logic, order, and a sense of comfort.

Why is the world round?

Why do humans exist?

Why is the sky blue?

Story. Story. Story.

What's the reason for all this explaining? See, I'm doing it now. The reason? Knowing provides a sense of comfort, perhaps even safety.

Knowing beats the heck out of the alternative. Not knowing brings feelings of confusion and disorder. It's no exaggeration to say that all the anthropological sciences exist to help us understand ourselves (humanity) better.

The unknown is frightening.

Confusion, chaos, and disorder can create mental discord.

Thus, it's little surprise that our thinking – particularly our personal narratives (stories) – plays a massive role in the evolution of our wellness and peace of mind.

But here's a crucial and somewhat frightening revelation: Our stories don't have to be accurate to provide comfort and safety. They don't even have to be factual. If they exist, and we believe them, they provide comfort.

However, there's a third alternative in the middle of the knowledge-story spectrum. This third alternative exists between knowing (comfort and safety) and the unknown (fear and confusion); it's a powerful *awareness*.

It's the recognition found in this simple, four-word sentence: "I do not know."

Give it a try: "I do not know."

How does that feel?

Interestingly, "I do not know" offers a sense of peace via acceptance. It acknowledges that most of our life and world is far beyond our comprehension.

Try it one more time:

"I do not know."

"I do not know"

KNOWN
Comfortable & Safe

*Acceptence
Peace of mind*

THE UNKNOWN
Uncomfortable & Frightening!

everythingastory.com

Mark Twain put it this way: "I was gratified to be able to answer promptly, and I did. I said I didn't know."

Socrates was far more direct: "I am the wisest man alive, for I know one thing, and that is that I know nothing."

Tragically, it's the know-it-all who is truly confused.

Paradox once again rearing its ugly and paradoxically beautiful head, leading us to a new appreciation of Lao Tzu's sparkling observation: "The words of truth are always paradoxical." (Although I suspect he actually said, "almost always.")

Then, there's one of my favorite characters from the Netflix series *Ozark*, Ruth Langley. Ruth shares her very similar, magnificent declaration, one that fits astonishingly well with this book's theme:

"I don't know sh*t about f*ck."

Whether it's Ruth Langley, Mark Twain, or Socrates (a bizarre trio, to be sure), the awareness is the same. If we're being truthful, we really don't know sh*t about f*ck more often than not.

No matter how much you know, there will always be far more you don't know and much more that you'll never know.

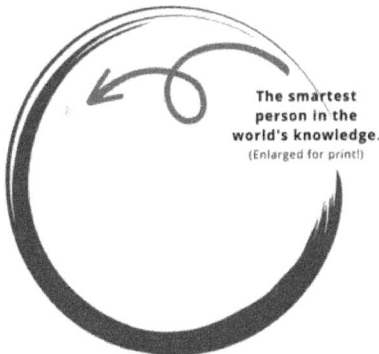

The smartest person in the world's knowledge.
(Enlarged for print!)

All knowledge!

everythingastory.com

Recently, a buddy caught me off-guard as we exited a restaurant and headed for our cars. "Man, it's all just so confusing, isn't it? I mean, I have my religion and my faith, but there are just so many questions. I enjoy discussing these things with you."

It was an unexpected exchange seconds from our car, hardly an ideal time to start a potentially long, philosophical conversation.

Knowing we had little time to discuss the matter, I left him with the third alternative: "I don't know, Andy, maybe these are things we're just not supposed to have the answers to."

How's that for a story?

"Ha!" he responded with light laughter and a bit of relief. "Maybe you're right."

***

In personal development, few lessons are as important as understanding your "*WHY?*" As in, *why* do you want to become a doctor? *Why* do you want to run a marathon? Or, *why* the f*ck do you get out of bed in the morning?

Understanding your *why* is as essential to goal achievement as it is to experiencing joy and a fulfilling life. Friedrich Nietzsche, the renowned German philosopher, noted, "He who has a why to live for can endure almost any how."

One can "endure any how" because they have meaning – purpose – and a sincere commitment to a specific outcome.

Your *why* is a powerful story that will inspire you to keep pressing on long after most quit.

Your why *story* underscores your desire – perhaps the most important ingredient in the pursuit of your goals and ideals and, not coincidentally, habit and skill development.

A powerful why story will push you through, over and around all the obstacles that will present themselves in pursuing your goals. Consider the artist who paints brilliantly *without* hands. Their desire is so intense they developed new skills and habits. (Holding the brush and painting with their feet).

When it comes to habit and skill development, three elements are necessary: desire, knowledge, and the essential capacity to perform the behavior.

Most of the time, sincere *desire* is the only missing ingredient.

A compelling why story is all you need to be committed in belief and deed.

Without a good *why* story – a purpose – life becomes dull or, worse, meaningless. However, with a compelling why and a captivating, meaningful story, life becomes extraordinarily important, profound, and purposeful. Your *why story* makes all the difference.

Why do you get out of bed?

Why are you pursuing that career?

Why are you working and practicing on becoming a doctor, rock star, chef, or cop?

Why do you want to learn how to play guitar?

Why are you building an app, writing a book, or becoming a bodybuilder? The list of potential *whys* is endless.

Have you ever heard the saying, "Chips on your shoulders can put chips in your pocket?"[28] It's a potent way to underscore how one can spin an emotionally charged *why* story in their favor.

Steph Curry is a four-time NBA championship winner who's already set the NBA's all-time three-point scoring record (with many more years to play). He's also a certain first-ballot hall-of-famer. Yet not everyone believed in him initially. Steph likely was – and maybe still is – fueled by all the early NBA scouts who went on the record with pronouncements like, "Stephen's explosiveness and athleticism are below standard...Do not rely on him to run your team."

Hah!

Whose story did Steph subscribe to?

Can you imagine what his *why* story sounds like?

"Undersized? Below standard athleticism? Not quick or explosive? Can't lead a team? I will show them who Stephen Curry is!"

"I can't wait for these 'experts' to eat their words. Stephen Curry will become the best shooting/point/combo-guard of all time!"

---

[28] Attributed to several sources.

Does a meaningful why story assure success? Absolutely not. There are thousands, maybe millions, of athletes with powerful *why* stories who never make it to the professional ranks. While a sincere desire is essential, it's only part of the equation.

Consider the 3 Circles of Behavior Echo-System, and it's easy to see how such a story at your core drives intense, emotional buy-in and fuels passionate training and practice habits (middle circle).

Even if Stephen Curry were to discount the "chip on his shoulder" story, as many athletes do, rest assured there is another meaningful story driving his habits and skills. Perhaps it's about becoming the greatest shooter of all time. Perhaps it's about "not reaching his peak" – meaning he has more to prove.

Simon Sinek, bestselling author and professional speaker, presented a fascinating Ted Talk[31] (2014, 56 million views) on "How leaders inspire action." In this talk, he emphasized the unforgettable message that *why* should be a business leader's first tenet.

Sinek says that the first story a business leader must effectively convey is why the company exists. When they do this effectively, business leaders will enjoy happier employees and loyal customers. Sinek's bestseller *Start with Why* underscores the same theme.

It follows that your why story is a core requirement to help fuel success. In fact, your *why* stories underscore and inspire all your *who*, *what*, and *where* stories.

Why do you want to become that particular *who*? *Why* do you want that particular *what*? Why do you want to go to that *where*? Your *why* story is behind it all.

***

Let's try a quick imagination exercise we'll call "Operation Time Travel." You get to travel back in time. As an example, let's say you possess Irish heritage and decide to visit Ireland in the 16th century.

You understand that life was tough then, but you view the period as a "simpler time." You love the idea of farming and living off the land, small communities, and zero traffic!

Upon arrival, you quickly realize there is no running water or plumbing and certainly no electricity or internet. No cell phones – zero technology!

You begin to question your decision.

The good news is that you can tell anyone you wish about the future.

You start by telling your great (to the power of [20-ish]) Uncle Randall McDermott that the future is astounding! Other family members gather around – they can sense your enthusiasm. You tell Randall that there will be tremendous advancements in farming, machinery, communications, travel, and medicine. You explain super-cool gadgets like the cell phone and flying drones.

The more you talk about the magical, wonderous future and all its technological advancements, the more you notice your relatives lose interest. Before you know it, everyone is gone. They're not just suspicious of what you're saying; they're questioning your sanity.

You finally realize that there is no way your 16th-century relatives can comprehend or even envision the *very real* technological advancements of the 21st century.

Here's the next part of the imagination exercise: Consider how you'd react if someone arrived from 500 years in the future and began explaining to you that in the future, humans live on average 229 years and that hunger hasn't been an issue since 2069. Most people don't have jobs, almost all work is creative, and robots perform all manual labor. Further, anyone can travel from the moon to Mars in just a few hours.

Would you believe them?

Is that scenario any different from telling people in the 16th century that you can travel more than halfway around the world in less than 16 hours on a jet plane? Consider how ludicrous that statement would sound if you were on a farm in the 16th century!

Sir Arthur Charles Clarke was an English science-fiction writer, futurist, inventor, undersea explorer, and television series host who famously observed, "Any sufficiently advanced technology is indistinguishable from magic."

Magic?

What is magic?

Let's begin by using its "near antonym," according to Merriam Webster, "science."

How's that for a riddle?

One more time, Arthur C. Clark: "Any sufficiently advanced technology is indistinguishable from magic."

What a beautiful conundrum!

Science leads us to seemingly "magical" inventions that are incomprehensible and impossible to explain until some future period. And imagination (magical thinking) leads us to create these scientific advancements.

According to Albert Einstein, imagination is "more important than knowledge." This observation comes from a man responsible for numerous scientific breakthroughs.

Imagination (thinking magically) is often the source of scientific breakthroughs, not its antithesis. And spirituality is often disregarded as silly or magical. Yet it was the legendary scientist, cosmologist, and astrophysicist Carl Sagan who affirmed, "Science is not only compatible with spirituality; it is a profound source of spirituality."

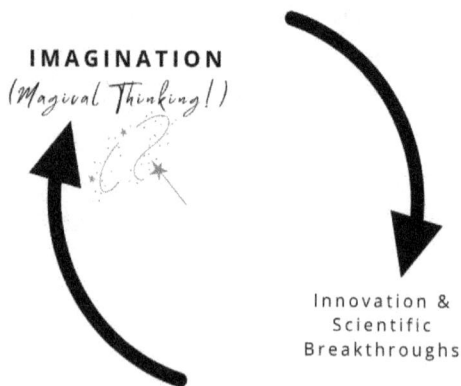

IMAGINATION
(Magical Thinking!)

Innovation &
Scientific
Breakthroughs

everythingastory.com

After all, empiricism, a philosophy that promotes knowledge as based exclusively upon sensory experience, doesn't account very well for the role imagination plays in human existence – in particular, all the imaginative stories we tell ourselves that tend to be devoid of actual sensory experience.

Why all the discussion around imagination and magic? Once again, we'll take our cue from Einstein: "Your imagination is your preview of life's coming attractions."

Here's another reason: Imagination creates possibilities, and possibilities create hope.

If your life is filled with troubles and you feel overwhelmed with problems, the first thing to consider is: Can you envision a way out?

One's lifeline is often tied to their horizon line.

Sometimes things are so bad and life is so sh*ty that the horizon line may just be "the next three hours," as my friend battling cancer explained following months of radiation and chemotherapy.

Martin Luther King, Jr. used to say, "You don't have to see the entire staircase; just take the first step."

Either way, it's imperative that you do see something new, better, and different and that you move in that direction.

Recall Jim Rohn's observation: "The good news is that ten years from now, you will surely arrive. The question is, where?"

What do the next few hours, days, or weeks look like? What does an ideal, positive future look like five or 10 years from now?

Ronald Reagan and a handful of politicians to follow have employed the "shining city upon a hill" reference in many of their speeches. *Why?* It's a hopeful, visual cue designed to tap into an audience's imagination; it's a beacon of hope.

Imagination and creativity are the roots of problem-solving. If you're reading or listening to this book on a device that isn't an old-fashioned book, how do you think that device came to be?

Imagination→ Creativity.

Further, *why* was the device created? What purpose did imagination play in its creation?

Vision, imagination, and creativity precede *all* advances.

For this reason, it's essential to affirm and cultivate your vision daily. Your capacity to imagine a better, more hopeful future while creating supportive stories fosters the values, decisions, actions, and behaviors (habits) that will carry you there.

As a creature, arguably, your first responsibility is to *create.*

Creation begins with imagination.

Our *why* stories fuel that creation.

Speaking of creation, have you ever wondered *why* you were born? Even if you keep that analysis strictly factual, were you able to follow the bouncing ball? While you may be able to explain your existence up to a certain point, depending upon how far back in time you go, there is an inexplicable element of chance. At what point does *your* existence fall into the lap of pure chance?

Why, for instance, did Grandma meet Grandpa at the high school dance? Well, it turns out that Grandma's original date was home sick. All life, including yours, rests *not* upon logic, reason, or science – that would be too reasonable and easy to explain.

Instead, the foundation of *everything* (creation, the universe, our planet, *your life*) rests upon the very "stuff" humans can only "explain" with imagination and stories.

At a certain point, logic, reason, and science (above all) run into a roadblock – a dead-end – forcing us back to the very beginning: imagination and creativity.

Consider this: From millions or even billions of possible stories, your *why* stories are yours alone, and each story was *created*. Others may lead you toward meaningful and purposeful *why* stories, but you alone determine whether you'll subscribe to them.

While most people consider their *why* stories to be a test of logic and reason, more often than not, they're a test of your imagination and creativity.

WHEN?

"Today is the eighth day of the month.
Tomorrow is the thirteenth."
~Zen koan

I read that ridiculous koan and marched out of my office into the general area, where we have a magnetic dart board. Fortunately for me, nobody was around to witness the lunacy. Otherwise, they might've called for the people with straitjackets.

A Zen koan is a quizzical and paradoxical statement intended to be meditated upon for days, weeks, perhaps even months, or years. By design, koans are meant to train the mind (typically for Zen Buddhist monks) to abandon their learned dependence upon reason and logic to force sudden, intuitive insight and enlightenment.

I lined up about eight feet from the dartboard, holding three magnetic darts. I repeated the koan aloud: "Today is the eighth day of the month. Tomorrow is the thirteenth!"

With each dart I threw, I repeated the koan and grew increasingly frustrated.

I collected the darts and lined up again.

"Ha! Today is the eighth day of the month. Tomorrow is the thirteenth!"

I began laughing like a madman.

I lined up for a third time for three more shots.

"This koan is total bullsh*t!"

I threw the first dart and landed much closer to the bullseye. I hit 18 on the inside third near the center.

"Today is the eighth day of the month. Tomorrow is the thirteenth!" I tossed the second dart. It landed on the black area, just outside the red bullseye.

I was practically yelling, "This koan makes ZERO sense!"

I threw my final dart, shouting, "It's completely NONSENSICAL!"

Bullseye!

Time: Is there anything more mysterious?

Einstein's famous observation encapsulates time's peculiar nature: "Put your hand on a hot stove for a minute, and it seems like an hour. Sit with a pretty girl for an hour, and it seems like a minute."

Time can be seemingly *everything*. It can be incredibly important, *and* it can be nothing.

It depends.

When it comes to pursuing your goals and ideals, one can make the case that *when* you achieve them matters far less than you may originally think (most of the time). In personal development circles, this is an unpopular opinion, but let me explain.

Does it really matter *when* you learn to play the piano? Maybe.

Does it really matter if you learn to paint this year or next? Maybe.

I thought I had to learn to kitesurf well before I was 50; I learned at 52. I thought this book had to be published in 2020 because the story I was telling myself is that each book in this "trilogy" had to be five years apart. It turns out that 2020 was a bad year for many things, publishing included. Further, it turns out this book is far better for the delay.

When NASA misses a launch date, it doesn't panic and certainly doesn't quit. It resets the schedule and keeps moving toward its goal. Few organizations are more goal-directed than NASA.

The reality is that we can and should manage our goals' deadlines accordingly. After all, some things are within our control, and many things are not.

Thus, Einstein's lessons apply spectacularly to goal achievement: Time is relative.

Incredibly, the case can be made that arriving at your goals later – procrastinating along the way – increases innovation and creativity.[32]

I recall being disappointed with myself that our Certified Professionals Program (THF-CPP) was delayed by years as I spent time and attention on books and other projects. Unbeknownst to me, those books and projects would end up making the certification program *more* valuable to our professionals.

Since goal achievement exists on a spectrum of probability, one of the best ways to enhance that probability is to simply slide the deadline to the right (adding time) *when* appropriate. Thus, the unexpected, much-regretted delay has the potential to become advantageous.

My friend John, the entrepreneur battling cancer, recently shared this in our mastermind: "I've been 4-6 weeks away from selling our company for the last three years. Finally! It's a done deal!" Delayed by years, he pulled off the sale of his company while fighting leukemia (treatments included chemo, radiation, and a bone marrow transplant) – a remarkable feat.

Once again, notice the power of both: It's important to set a deadline and, if necessary, to extend the deadline.

Unfortunately, most people often fail to set an initial deadline because of the pain (pressure) it would create. Then, if they set a deadline that passes, instead of appreciating their progress, they quit.

Think about that: quitting because of a self-imposed, arbitrary deadline?

Who would do such a thing?

For years, I've taught something I like to call "the accordion method" (apply pressure and then release it). It works as well for creativity as for goal achievement and productivity.

As I write this, I'm scrambling to go to Indonesia for a surf odyssey around the Mentawai islands. The number of "things" I've had to accomplish leading up to my departure seemed improbable, and there was just one reason they were all accomplished: **a deadline.**

Knowing I'd be mostly without internet access for nearly three weeks forced me to be hyper-focused. Deadlines create pressure – potentially good, positive pressure if we plan, prepare, and practice appropriately. So, it's essential to set a deadline, but sometimes, it's essential to extend it.

People arrive in our automaticgoals.com program and think 28 days is too long to "get" where they want to go. Once in the program, they realize that 28 days is just the beginning of the process.

If it takes 10 years to finish your novel, so be it. It was 10 years spent pursuing an ideal. In the end, how much will it matter that it took 10 years vs. three years?

Who knows?

One thing we know about time: It's going to pass anyway, so you may as well be on the path, directing your time and energy toward a meaningful, worthwhile goal.

The short story is that when it comes to pursuing your goals, everyone works with the same raw material – just one day at a time, no more, no less.

Brian Tracy loves to draw the analogy of a delivery truck backing up to your home each morning to deliver 24 fresh, beautiful new hours directly to your doorstep. With each

new set of 24 hours, the corresponding ingredients –
opportunity and hope – arrive in unison.

One of my favorite adages – not to mention images – is
"Festina lente." It's the Latin, paradoxical phrase that,
loosely translated, means "make haste, slowly." It's
sometimes conveyed in English as "more haste, less speed."

The representative image is a dolphin wrapped around
an anchor. Apparently, emperors Augustus and Titus were
so enraptured by the phrase that they had its image
imprinted upon coins.

33

Festina lente is a wise reminder that our time is limited. Thus, it's imperative to live with a sense of urgency while at the same time retaining our equilibrium.

The beauty is this: Festina lente could be the motto of The Habit Factor, as it parallels its philosophy to a tee.

The Habit Factor demands users identify their essential life goals and ideals (because life is short). At the same time, it teaches that the path to each goal can't be rushed. It requires the cultivation of core, related habits.

In short, Festina lente simply says: "Hey f*ck-face, you're going to die. That is certain! What isn't certain is how well you are going to live. What's your legacy story going to be? How are you going to use your precious time?"

John Wooden, legendary UCLA Bruin head basketball coach (1948-1975), must've been a fan of Festina lente. He was often heard yelling to his players, "Be quick, but don't hurry." [34]

Festina lente is a straightforward reminder for balancing our decisions and actions with speed (urgency) while remaining calm and poised; to move methodically toward our goals and ideals.

Another favorite axiom from Brian Tracy is this: "There is always enough time to do the most important things, and there is never enough time to do everything." The statement underscores the significance of our choices, decisions, and strategies.

What are the most significant decisions in your life? It's tough to argue that they're not the Who, What, Where, and even Why stories.

The When story is almost always less important, subservient to your life's Who, What, Where, and Why? stories.

Here's another question: When are you going to die?

The honest answer is very few people know precisely when they will die. Yet, everyone knows they will die.

Thus, the question's value isn't in its answer; it's in the related exploration and conceptualization – the stories that arise.

While very few know precisely when they will die, what's the one thing everyone alive possesses equally?

Now!

It's a bit cliché within the personal development space to encourage only mindfulness at the expense of reflecting upon your past or considering an uncertain future. I wholeheartedly encourage all the above (in balance, of course).

After all, a regretful story of a past decision or action can foster the wisdom (hopefully) to guide us to better actions and decisions in the future.

A story for another day, perhaps, but I can assure you my books exist because of such reflection – because of many poor decisions and actions as an adolescent.

Yet, we shouldn't dwell for days, weeks, or months in the emotion of regret. Instead, we should observe and preserve the lesson. "When you lose," the Dalai Lama advises, "don't lose the lesson."

The emotion of regret possesses valuable lessons, making Aristotle's observation worth repeating: "Wisdom is equal measure experience plus reflection." Reflection can offer a path to a better future.

Further, with foresight, we can investigate a potentially troublesome, worrisome future, anticipate undesirable outcomes, and, in theory, make course corrections *now*.

If your vessel is headed toward the rocks, the only sensible thing to do is to correct course, and the best time to do that is now.

Foresight also provides the ambitious sailor a way to capitalize on future opportunities by noticing trends and tailwinds and asking *where* they may lead in the future.

Mindfulness (being only in the present moment) does not provide that luxury.

I recount the following story in *The Habit Factor*.

***

The other day, my 7-year-old daughter Eva asked her mother, "Mommy, when is the future created?"

This, it turned out, was one gem of a question – an unintentional, real-life Zen koan that my wife shared with me. She said, rather perplexed, "I wasn't sure what to tell her."

I realized that I had no response either to my daughter's question. Stumped, I decided that I would sleep on it. "When is the future created?" I kept asking myself. What a great question. I even posted it on Facebook to see what my friends thought. One friend suggested I tell Eva, "Tomorrow! Tell her the future is created tomorrow."

Forty-eight hours later, the answer hit me:

NOW!

That's it! The future is created now! There is no tomorrow, and there is no yesterday. The only moment we all have is *now*. I'm sure we all recognize this on some level, but how many of us have contemplated its significance? It is so significant, in fact, that the great Zen master Seng-ts'an once proclaimed, "No tomorrow. No today. No yesterday." There can only be NOW. Thank you, Eva and Seng-ts'an.

Such an awakening should provide everyone with a tremendous reprieve. Reflect on that for a moment: It makes literally no difference how "bad" yesterday, last week, last year, or even today was. The last 10 years or 10 seconds don't matter. The future (your future) is created now. And now, I remind you, is where habit is listening very intently, recording your present energies (thoughts and actions) right at this moment.

***

Now is when your future is created!

NOW holds all the magic, all the stories (past, present, and future), and all the potential required to create your ideal future. Do you believe it? Can you see it?

You may be saying, "Yes! But how?"

"How?" is the next chapter. We've covered the first two keys: employing your imagination and harnessing the power of now!

Now, let's continue the journey.

HOW?

"Awareness is like the sun; when it shines on things, they are transformed."
~Thich Nhat Hanh

In Ernest Hemingway's classic 1926 novel, *The Sun Also Rises*, the following exchange takes place:
"How did you go bankrupt?" Bill asked.
"Two ways," Mike said. "Gradually and then suddenly."

The last of the six stories that really freakin' matter is: "How?"
How will you "arrive" at your "success"? How are you going to create your ideal future?

Arguably, the only way anyone ever arrives anywhere is via the supreme, natural "law" of "gradually, and then suddenly."

Gradually, and then suddenly, is how a large oak tree comes into existence. Gradually, then suddenly, is how anyone becomes old. Barring inheritance, gambling, or lottery winnings, gradually, then suddenly, is how most people become rich. Gradually, then suddenly.

Should the world end, that is precisely how it will unfold: gradually, and then suddenly.

This "law" applies to nearly everything, from going bankrupt to gaining or losing weight to growing tomatoes – it's an inescapable law of nature noticeable *everywhere*.

Importantly, this law is as much a process as a roadmap. If you're training to complete your first marathon, you can rest assured the training will be slow and gradual. It will hurt, and there will be much resistance. Then, race day will arrive, and because you have planned, prepared, and practiced accordingly, you will cross the finish line. Suddenly, you are a marathoner!

Grasping this law helps anyone adopt the crucial mindset that all becoming is a perpetual process that demands patience.

Henry David Thoreau underscored this awareness with the following stunning declaration:

"If one advances confidently in the direction of [their] dreams, and endeavors to live the life which [they have] imagined, [they] will meet with a success *unexpected in common hours*."

"To meet with a success unexpected in common hours" is sudden. To pursue your dreams confidently and "endeavor to live the life you imagined" is slow and gradual; it only occurs one day at a time.

It doesn't matter if you're training to become a doctor, teacher, or farmer. Each profession demands patience, effort, and a sincere desire – a commitment to an envisioned outcome.

A crucial idea to remember is that goal achievement and personal transformation are often the same. For instance, if my goal is to become a medical doctor and I'm currently a mechanic (or vice-versa), I must develop new habits and skills. Knowledge isn't enough. It is applied knowledge, via effort and intentional practice, that produces well-formed habits and skills.

Ryan Hall retired in his mid-thirties as America's fastest marathoner, recording the fastest marathon (2:04:58) and half-marathon (59:43). Then, he decided to do something unique, particularly for distance runners – build up his physique.

As a competitive marathoner, Ryan weighed just 129 pounds. Today, Ryan Hall has "transformed himself into a functional fitness powerhouse" [35] who weighs 190 pounds. "When I started, I had a goal of benching, squatting, and deadlifting 300 pounds...now I'm benching 330, squatting 480, and deadlifting 530."

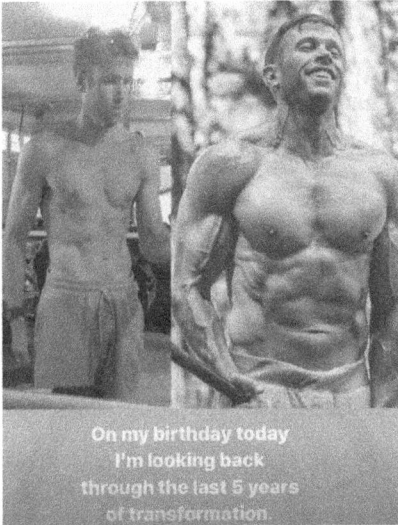

Image: @ryanhall3, Instagram. Five-year transformation!36

Ryan's story clearly demonstrates that *becoming* something new and different is a *metamorphosis*, which, by definition, often requires new habits (and skills). Worth repeating: Ryan had a clear goal – a vision of his desired outcome.

The question for us mortals is, *how* in the world is such an astounding personal transformation possible? One of the world's fastest marathoners transformed into a mini-Incredible Hulk, benching 330 pounds.

How?

Here's precisely how *anyone* achieves any goal involving personal transformation: new habits and skills.

Let's look at Ryan's transformation in the context of the 3 Circles of Behavior Echo-System (a simplified, innovative behavior model as discussed in the "Three Circles-The Redux" chapter).

everythingastory.com

Environment || Habits/Skills || Story/Mindset

214

Environment: How do you think Ryan's new environment (as a weightlifter) differs from his prior environment as a track star? Could you identify two or three different things in his new environment?

_____

_____

(For example, a weight training coach, research, videos, and instruction.)

Story/Mindset: What sort of story or mindset could be driving Ryan's vision? Can you guess one or two storylines Ryan subscribed to that drove his transformation?

_____

_____

For example: "I can't wait to experiment. I don't think this has been done before, and I think I can pull this off!" Remember, a Hero's mindset is always required: Hopeful, Empowered, Responsible & Optimistic!

Habits/Skills: Given Ryan's different environment and storylines, what habits and skills do you think he fostered that aided his metamorphosis? Could you guess two or three new habits and skills[29]?

_____

_____

For example, more calories and protein; changing his diet.

---

[29] Supportive skills and good habits require intentional practice.

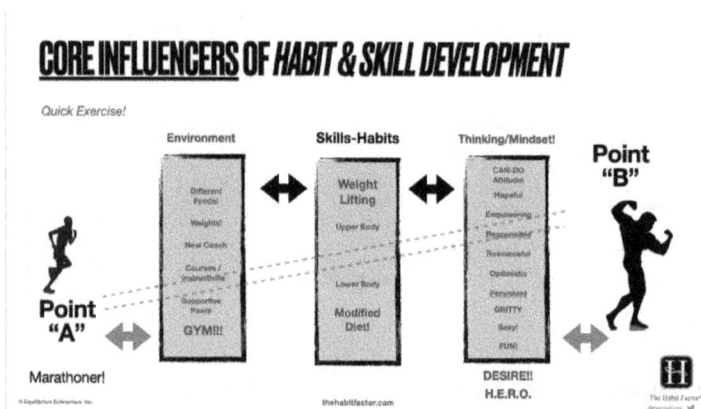

Image: Presentation, "Executive Coaching for Profound Transformation"

When it comes to *how* you will achieve your most meaningful goals, you must consider and involve *all three areas*: *Environment*, *Habits/Skills*, and *Story/Mindset*.

Here's a simplified example: Imagine a person who aspires to be an international public speaker; however, they're in prison. The prison – their environment – is a significant limiter, preventing them from realizing their goal (at least in the near term).

While their effort, practice, and skill/habit development may be excellent, their environment prevents them from realizing their goal.

A more complex variation: A professor (MBA, Ed.D.) I coached was contending with multiple personal situations, including an elderly parent to assist and an ongoing homeowner's association conflict. These in-state and out-of-state obligations disrupted his efforts to track the agreed-upon habits. In short, "life happened" to him.

That was his story. Reality or not, it's a story – one that influenced his emotions, behaviors, and decisions.

His environment and story were both unsupportive of his attempts to cultivate new habits. When this happens, it's a telling indicator, particularly for coaches or other behavior-change professionals, as it illuminates where incongruence or trouble may lie – either in one's stories or environment (more on this process in the next Section).

Related: This is where many coaches and behavior change professionals may struggle. They attempt to "fix" a client's problem by focusing exclusively on *one aspect instead of taking a holistic, three-pronged approach* and looking at Environment, Skills/Habits, and Story.

This sort of advice is prevalent on social media, YouTube, and throughout the internet. You may hear a thought leader, expert, or coach declaring, for instance, "It's *all* about *mindset!*" Unfortunately, they fail to appreciate or mention the other major components involved.

As recounted in the earlier "Failure" chapter, sometimes deeply buried stories cause misalignment; these stories may have been hiding for years, perhaps decades.

This raises a few related questions: If stories can remain hidden for so long, *how* do we know they exist? If we discover them, how do we rewrite a debilitating story?

Let's address these questions in order.

If you're unsure whether your stories are supportive of your goals and ideals (*where* you are trying to go and *what* you're trying to become), *there is only one place to look*:

Your results!

GIGO! Garbage in, garbage out. Greatness In. Greatness Out. Your outcomes – your results – are the lagging indicator of your efforts. Your daily activities and habits are the input.

Chance, accidents, and random events – things beyond our control – undoubtedly affect our situation, *and* we can choose *how* we respond.

It's both.

If you're prone to blaming accidents, circumstances, and generally sh*ty events for your life's *results,* you're encouraged to revisit the "Prolific" chapter.[37]

"The secret of change," Socrates insisted, "is to focus all of your energy not on fighting the old, but on building the new." This is precisely what The Habit Factor teaches. And this is precisely the answer to how you can improve and rewrite any debilitating story.[30]

Whether it's the cessation of thought or behavior habits, the essential key is *developing the new.* "A nail is driven out by another nail." Desiderius Erasmus, the Dutch philosopher from the 16th century, said, "Habit is replaced by habit."

As covered previously, just one storyline consumes your attention at any moment in time. It's essential to acknowledge that story and replace it immediately with a favorable one aligned with *where* you are trying to go.

---

[30] More on the process of rewriting debilitating stories in the "Application" section.

Sounds simple enough, right?

Simple, yes. Easy, no. Thomas Fuller – known as "Negro Tom" and the "Virginia Calculator" – was an enslaved African celebrated for his mathematical ability. He put it best when he said, "All things are difficult before they are easy."

What creates ease, over time, is practice: the *art* of practice. (More on that in the next chapter.) Once you've committed to developing any new habit or skill, the *tracking* must begin![31]

If, despite your best efforts and intentions to track, your habit-tracking data isn't materializing, you must investigate two places where the problem may lie: your *environment* and your *stories*.

You may be thinking, "Hold on! What about *feelings* and *emotions*? Aren't they essential to behavior, goal achievement, and personal transformation?"

Yes!

Feelings and emotions may be the most powerful influencers of our behaviors (decisions and actions), particularly from one moment to the next. *And*, notably (in theory anyway), adults can and should manage their emotions *most of the time*. After all, that is what emotional intelligence is.

Thus, when it comes to goal achievement and personal transformation, feelings and emotions are *minimized* within

---

[31] P.A.R.R. is how to track! Plan, Act, Record, and Reassess.

the 3 Circles of Behavior Echo-System. Recall that they are "conduits." Rather than representing core, significant influencers of our skills and habit development, their influence is minimized over the long haul.

Consider how Ryan Hall's feelings and emotions varied throughout his five-year journey into a "functional fitness powerhouse."[38] He started the quest as a 129-pound marathoner and morphed into a 190-pound powerhouse who benched 330 pounds.

His emotions and feelings *must have varied* from one day, week, and month to the next, over several years: He is human after all.

Ryan would undoubtedly encounter many highs – happy, optimistic, empowered, great days. He also likely endured many lows, where he was demotivated and discouraged.

Rest assured, "life happened" to Ryan, as it does to everyone who pursues long-term, worthwhile goals. Accidents, injuries, setbacks, tough days, etc., are all par for the course – part of the journey.

The key takeaway is that feelings and emotions are *ephemeral* – they are perpetually changing from one moment to the next.[32] Thus, with some awareness, we can and should manage our feelings most of the time.

Our environment and stories – our personal narratives over the long haul – most influence our habit and skill

---

[32] More on feelings and emotions in the "Application" section and Q&A.

development (which can take months or years). *Developing habits and skills prompts transformation and goal achievement.*

Reflect deeply for just a few minutes about your greatest achievement – the happiest, most uplifting, and joyful moment of your life. Put the book down; take a few minutes at least. Relish the memory. Recall that *story* in great detail.

Q: Do you feel happy?
A: Of course you do!
(That's a great story, by the way.)

I recently had lunch with one of the best business coaches I know. Braun told me he didn't uncover his most debilitating childhood story until he was 45, 15-plus years ago.

"What I discovered was that I had unconsciously accepted labels about myself. For instance, 'I was a coward who could not protect his mother.' I carried around a lot of guilt and shame."

It turns out that at just 4 or 5 years old, Braun was making too much noise, and his stepfather became abusive. "My mom stepped in the middle to protect me; I hid under the bed, praying to God to protect her. God didn't stop it, and I couldn't stop it."

"What led you to this story?" I asked. "Why were you searching and doing this sort of work?" "Well," Braun responded. "I began asking questions, wondering about my recurring patterns of behavior. I wasn't happy, and I really wasn't happy with my *results*."

His results were the first key indicator that something wasn't "right." So, Braun went searching. To his surprise, he uncovered a story that shaped his identity and influenced his behaviors (decisions, actions, habits, and skills).

Sharing Braun's *story* demonstrates how our identity – *who* we are and *what* we can achieve – is often forged at a very young age.

Such stories tend to go unnoticed until we begin to assess our results in the most elemental areas of our lives: health, relationships, finances, career, achievement, performance, etc.

These are the stories that are at the epicenter of our lives. They are the *hub* – the veritable helm – our life's steering wheel, directing our future path.

While Braun's story is difficult to hear, it's easy to see how decades of behaviors and *results* could be impacted if left unchecked.

Braun went on to say: "I went to work on myself. I was open to the process of discovery, and it really helped to have a professional (counselor) – a third party to help me discover the faulty programming that I'd created by carrying such a story around."

Another key: Since life is dynamic, each new day presents additional information, relationships, and challenges. Thus, we should never stop exploring our most important stories relative to their results.

Anytime you recognize that your recurring results don't match your goals and ideals, it's time to begin the discovery process – to audit all the related narratives.

Part of the story-excavation process involves a *why* archeological dig. Neuroscientists have recently observed that "thoughts act like worms." In fact, they call them "thought worms," representing transitions of thought.[39]

Similarly, an ancient Buddhist scripture, the Samyutta Nikaya, likens our thoughts to monkeys leaping from one branch to another, often without care or intention.

Either way, the essential idea is that as you begin to search your *whys*, the answers will present an underlying narrative. Therefore, it's crucial to ask *why* multiple times – some coaches say three times, some five; some say more. My experience is there is no set number. I suggest you keep asking *why* as often as possible until the answer keeps repeating itself, and you sense you've approached the one story that feeds the others, like a massive river feeding various streams.

Your first answer will almost always be superficial and insignificant. The next few answers will help you to connect the dots to a deeper, more meaningful story.

For instance, in one of my entrepreneur groups, a member couldn't figure out why she didn't care too much about growing her company. *Why?*

She thought it was that she didn't "need a lot of money." She *thought* it was because of her values; money wasn't a high value. Since values guide our behavior, she was right. Values possess underlying narratives as well. *And, of course, there was more to the story.*

It wasn't until she went through a series of *why* questions – something I like to call the "why worm-hole analysis" – that she discovered the real, underlying story. It was simple: Growing her business, she *believed* (she had a story for), would equate to less time with her child. (Sound familiar?)

I'm not interested in growing my company quickly!

Why?

More clients mean more headaches

I may lose existing clients...

We'll be short on resources

I'll have to work longer hours and harder...

I'll miss out on time with my son...

Haven't other executives and entrepreneurs managed growth and found ways to be there for their children?

everythingastory.com

Now, it's time for a pop quiz! It's a simple, one-question exam. You might even consider it a Zen koan.

Are you ready?

If *everything* is contained within the 3 Circles of Behavior Echo-System (and it is), what – if anything – is outside of it? Take a long look at the model:

This question has been asked many times, and nobody has gotten the answer right away. It may be helpful to recall that pain and curiosity are two essential keys to learning.

I can't recount the number of times my father had me in tears trying to teach me mathematics and science.

Hopefully, there will be no tears here: So, what, if anything, lies outside the 3 Circles of Behavior Echo-System if *everything* is inside it?

Meditate on that question, please.

We'll pick this up in the "Application" section.

APPLICATION

Fast and slow.
Certain and uncertain.
Strong and gentle.
The middle path is the way.

"Zen has no business with ideas."
~D.T. Suzuki

THE ART OF PRACTICE

"Intentional practice is at the heart of all growth and personal development."

Tears aside, did you figure it out?

What, if anything, exists outside the 3 Circles of Behavior Echo-System?

If *EVERYTHING* is located inside this Behavior Echo-System – your thoughts, behaviors, and even the all-inclusive environment, including people, your physical surroundings, and all your life's **inputs** and **outputs** – what could possibly be on the *outside?*

A riddle, indeed! A bit of a mind-bender.

Anyone?

Bueller?

The first and only clue you'll get is the opening quote of the last chapter from Thich Nhat Hanh.

That's it!

The answer is ***awareness***.

You may be saying, "Wait! Awareness is our thinking, and thought is clearly represented *within* the Three Circles of Behavior Echo-System."

Yes! Thought is inside, and when it is in the form of awareness, it's outside.

It's both!

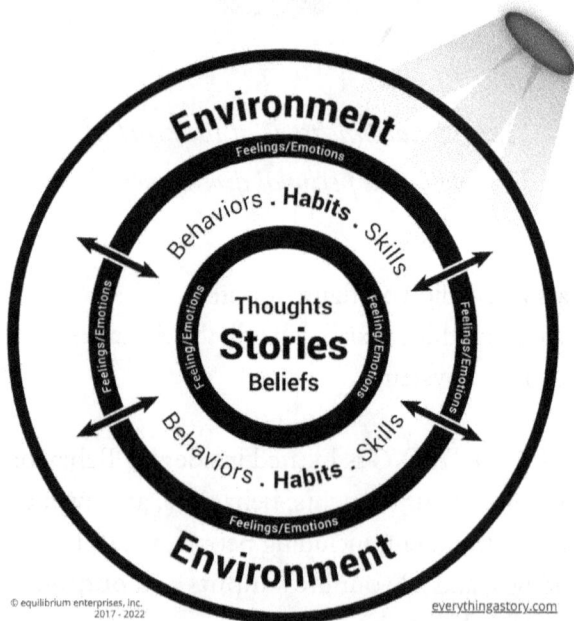

© equilibrium enterprises, inc.
2017 - 2022

everythingastory.com

When looking for something, particularly in the dark, you'd first bring a flashlight and shine its light from the outside.

The light is your awareness. Awareness allows us to observe the *entire* Behavior Echo-System (our thoughts, behaviors, and environment) from afar – detached.

From the beginning of our journey together, way back in the Preface, we spoke of "stepping off the train of thought" to observe *where* the train is headed.

As far as we know, there is just one creature with the unique capacity to separate itself from its own Behavior Echo-System.

Consider how powerful that is! That capacity alone may be your greatest superpower.

Theories abound about a handful of animals that may possess self-awareness. Yet, what other creature can detach and elevate its perspective with intention and assess its thoughts and behaviors to see if they align with future goals and ideals?

None. Only you can do this.

Just you, baby!

Further, by pausing and injecting awareness (adding time and space), humans can alter the Behavior Echo-System to change mere reactions to responses.

Environmental Stimulus → Reaction! Unhelpful & Undesired!

Environmental Stimulus — Pause — Response Helpful & Desired!

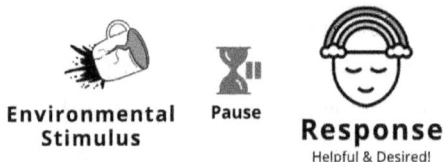

everythingastory.com

Responding is such a powerful skill that Viktor Frankl labeled it "the last of the human freedoms."

The Austrian Holocaust survivor, psychologist, and neurologist observed, "Between stimulus (what happens to us from our environment) and response (how we react), there is a space. In that space is our power to choose our response. *In our response lies our growth and our freedom.*"

Accordingly, our freedom and growth become *conditional* upon our awareness, which affords us an opportunity to respond rather than react. It's the act of *responding* that helps to cultivate harmony and wisdom.

Socrates *demanded* that we bring awareness to our life. In fact, he was callous in his observation:

"The unexamined life is not worth living."

Not worth living?!

Carl Jung underscored the importance of awareness saying, "Until you make the unconscious conscious, it will direct your life and you will call it fate."

With awareness, we improve our effectiveness by elevating our vantage point *above and beyond* the Behavior Echo-System. In so doing, we notice all our behaviors and stories and even their corresponding programs – our habits.

By stepping outside the Behavior Echo-System, we don't just assess the programs; technically, we can even assess the *programmer*.

How do you grade your programs? (Your habits.)

How do you grade the programmer? (You.)

That is awareness.

Is the programmer practicing new skills and cultivating new habits? Is the programmer learning new information to upgrade their skills? Are you sharpening the proverbial "saw," as Dr. Stephen Covey liked to say?

When all the primary areas of your life (Mind, Body, Social, and Spiritual) – including relationships, health (fitness and wellness), career, finances, lifestyle/adventure, and emotions – are all optimized and effective, providing the results you desire, give yourself an A.

The "truth" is, I've yet to meet anyone ever, even the greatest of Personal Development Goo-Roos, who have every dimension of their life operating *simultaneously* at its highest level. Typically, something gives; there is only so much energy and attention to go around at any one moment in time.[33]

Having said that, awareness affords anyone the essential insight to address areas that need attention. Feeling off-balance is akin to your car's check-engine light turning on. It's a signal that it's time to put your attention elsewhere.

While all the areas of your life may not be operating at peak efficiency simultaneously, it is possible, over time, to optimize and improve each.

A subtle but essential distinction mentioned previously relative to the Behavior Echo-System is that anything "outside" of your thinking is considered an environmental influencer. Thus, your body is an environmental factor, as it is separate from your thinking, emotions, feelings, and behaviors.

For instance, say I wake up *feeling* achy. My body relays information that affects my thoughts, feelings, and emotions. Thus, my behavior is changed; maybe I say something like, "I don't feel very well." Then, I walk downstairs looking for aspirin.

---

[33] See "Balance Wheel" in the "Practice & Exercises" section.

Armed with this knowledge, what do you think will guide and influence a lifetime of your decisions, actions, and behaviors environmentally?

Since you'll be sailing your vessel, that ought to be clue enough.

Is your ship watertight? Is it ship shape? Are there any leaks? Is it well-maintained? Is it seaworthy? Do you think your vessel can withstand a lifetime of challenging storms?

Apologies for the extended list of cliches, yet they couldn't be more fitting.

Warren Buffet, the world's most successful investor, enjoys telling students, "Let's pretend I'm going to buy you a brand-new car. It's the car of your dreams, and it'll be waiting for you when you get home. There's just one catch," he cautions. "It's the only car you will have for the rest of your life."

How's that for awareness?

Couple that awareness with the 3 Circles of Behavior Echo-System model, and you have both a map and a compass. Once you know *where* you want to go, it's far easier to see *how* you will arrive.

The Polish American philosopher and scientist Alfred Korzybski noted, "The map is not the territory."

At a certain point, each of us must roll up our sleeves, put down our plans, and set sail (see the "Where?" chapter). We must leave anchor. We must advance into unchartered territory, developing new skills and habits along the way. *This* chapter shows you precisely how to turn this model into a *framework*.

The very first step is to enter the territory.

Understanding that goal achievement and personal transformation actuate within the middle layer (habits and skills) is crucial.

Thus, the intentional *practice* of daily habit tracking (more days than not) is how one enters the territory.

Tracking a few core supportive habits that will move you daily toward your goals and ideals is simple.

Unfortunately, most people who read this will never track. #truestory

We'll review why that is in the next chapter, "Mastery."

For those committed to pursuing their goals and developing the necessary habits and skills, check out the following step-by-step process.

***

How to put the Behavior Echo-System into action:

It begins with the intentional practice of daily habit tracking.

STEP #1:
Do you have a compelling "Why?"

Desire is the most critical ingredient for habit and skill development and goal achievement. So, what is your desire story? Have you written it out? Can you list several reasons why the required habits and skills are critical to developing this goal? What does your commitment story sound like?

Yes or **No** (circle one)

If it's a no, that's OK. Sleep on it. Give it a day, a week, or even a month or two. Recall Confucius's enlightened observation: "You have two lives, and the second one begins the moment you realize you only have one."

Take a month or two or six to identify your most important goal. Realize there is only so much time, and you'll adjust your course along the way, anyway.[34]

STEP #2:
Are you habit tracking?

---

[34] If you're still struggling with your desire and "Why?" story, chances are good you haven't done the exercises mentioned at the beginning: Obituary, Rocking Chair, or Bucket List.

I never like to say "must," as in you *must* do something. Having said that, if your goal is important, you *must* track your habits.

You may be thinking, "A lot of people have experienced success without habit tracking." First, don't be so sure. I can nearly guarantee they were doing some form of tracking. Second, the presumption is that you're reading this book for some guidance; here it is.

Track your f'n habits, *please*.

Here are the 3D's of why you must track habits:

Habit-tracking provides proof of your **DESIRE** backed by your attention and intention from one day to the next. Additionally, habit tracking provides the **DATA** necessary to see where you are headed. Finally, the act of tracking will help to cultivate the habit of **DISCIPLINE**.

While we can trace the art of habit tracking as far back as our buddy Benjamin Franklin, and perhaps even earlier, the popularity of habit tracking for goal achievement (apps and journals) can be traced to The Habit Factor's inception in 2009 (app). The book's subtitle reveals its age: "An innovative method to align habits with goals to achieve success."

Today the number of books and apps that espouse these ideas is in the thousands. In 2009, The Habit Factor was alone.

Unfortunately, somewhere along the way, the reasons to track habits and the process itself have become bastardized.

Today, it's common to notice silly ideas in the form of tweets and blog posts proclaiming things like, "habits and systems are better than goals."[35]

It's almost like that exercise where 10 people line up to pass along a message. As the message moves from one person to the next, it changes.

Habits and goals complement each other. Goals provide the target and desired outcome; habits provide the daily input to realize the goal.

As far as the process of habit tracking goes, a less effective habit-tracking method is to simply put a dot or "X" next to a behavior or habit for the day and move on. Something like this:

How NOT to habit track...

everythingastory.com

---

[35] A collection of daily habits is a *routine*, not a system. A "system" is a set of environmental resources that facilitate habits and skills. A franchise, for instance, implements *systems* to help foster employee habits and skills that support company goals.

While that form of habit tracking is better than nothing, it's not ideal.

The Habit Factor's P.A.R.R. method for habit tracking is significant for many reasons, including how it promotes the development of *habitstrength* and *automaticity* from one four-week tracking period to the next. P.A.R.R employs tracking parameters, including Target Days, Minimum Success Criteria, and Tracking Periods.

By tracking in successive, four-week "Tracking Periods," you strengthen the behavior's "automaticity," a scientific term identifying a behavior that requires little or no conscious thought. Hence, they become habits.

The above-illustrated habit tracker does little to denote target days. For instance, should you attempt the habit every day or just Monday, Wednesday, and Friday? There's no minimum success criteria: Are you attempting 15 pushups or 50? Finally, it doesn't address tracking periods: Should you track for a week or month? What happens next month?

As there are dozens of reference points online and an entire book, *The Habit Factor*, dedicated to this recommended method of habit tracking, we won't review the P.A.R.R. method in its entirety here. Instead, when you're ready, visit The Habit Factor's downloadable templates.[40]

Once you're committed to habit tracking, your journey has begun! Congratulations!

So: Are you habit tracking?

Yes or **No** (circle one)

To improve results in any area, you must gather data. Tracking your behaviors and habits creates precious data by forcing the intentional cultivation of a habit or skill. This data signifies if you're ON or OFF track each day!

BTW: Those two phrases, "on-track" and "off-track," should be clue enough that tracking your habits and intentional practice are *essential*.

Even knowing that you are off-track is helpful. Further, being off-track often points us to where within the Behavior Echo-System something else may be askew, for example, your *environment* or *story*.

Important: The practice of intentional habit tracking will highlight any other areas within the Behavior Echo-System that may be problematic.

Further, habit tracking will let you know if you're tracking the wrong habits or even if your goal has changed.

Related story: I was working with an entrepreneur in his mid-40s to achieve his goal of completing his first half-Ironman. He trained for just over four months and became well-conditioned and fit. Gary was well on his way to accomplishing his goal. However, as race day approached, he realized his actual goal was to become more fit, not compete in any event. By having a goal and tracking his habits, he realized that his *actual* goal was to be more fit.

Habit Tracking?

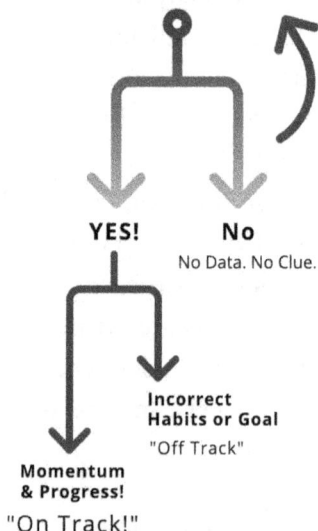

YES!   **No**

No Data. No Clue.

**Incorrect
Habits or Goal**

"Off Track"

**Momentum
& Progress!**

"On Track!"

everythingastory.com

STEP #3:
Are you gathering habit-tracking data?
Is habit tracking happening? If not, why not?

1. Habit-tracking is happening! Positive results and nearly instant momentum toward a goal!

On-track!

2. Habit-tracking is not happening! This is good information! Discouraging results related to habit tracking means you're *off-track!*

It's time to assess if the problem is A, B, or C:

A) Desire: Does your desire story truly exist?
Despite someone's belief that their desire story is
sufficient and compelling, the tracking data proves
otherwise. This is common.

Example: I really wanted to track this week, but I
forgot. I really wanted to track this week, but I was
super busy. I really wanted to track this week, but
my dog ate my homework.

Each is a clear indicator that no sincere
commitment or desire story exists.

If the desire story is meaningful and isn't the
problem, then it's time to look at the excuse stories.

B) Environmental challenges. The excuses
(stories) are related to real environmental challenges.
Desire and commitment exist! Unfortunately, so do
real environmental challenges.

Example: I really wanted to track my habits this
week, but my car was stolen. I really wanted to track
this week, but our dog died, my child was sick, we
suffered a hurricane, etc. If this happens, you simply
reset when the environment becomes favorable

again. Give it another week or month – however long it takes to get "back on track!"

C) Strategy is faulty: Your strategy is the final piece to assess. The tracking momentum is moving you *somewhere*, just not where you wanted to go. Here we typically find that someone is tracking the "wrong" habits or skills.

Example: A business owner whose goal is "more sales in the fourth quarter" elects to focus on copywriting as a habit to track. It turns out it makes more sense to outsource copywriting; the owner's time would be better spent cultivating relationship-building habits.

Importantly, you'll only realize you're off course after gathering some genuine feedback (habit-tracking data.)

Worth mentioning: A good business coach would likely have guided the business owner to identify more effective habits to track in the first place.[41]

Goal achievement and personal development are explorations. Exploration requires data. Habit-tracking provides the critical data to determine whether you're on track or off-track.

Consider that all types of captains – pilots, sailors, adventurers, explorers, even Captain Kirk from *Star Trek* – keep logs or journals.

A journal provides the essential data that helps them determine where they're going, assess progress, and learn lessons.

Did you notice that Benjamin Franklin kept a journal? Did you notice that good ol' Ben tracked his habits?

You may be saying, "Well, BF was a legend, a genius, a great man – an author, inventor, and founding father of the U.S. of A! I'm just an average Joe. I don't need to keep a journal!"

Tell me: Was Benjamin Franklin great before or after he started keeping his journal? Did Ben Franklin become a great man before or after he started tracking his habits?

Sidenote: That's a crappy, non-serving story that you're telling yourself about yourself.

Is that really the identity story you want to *carry* around? "I'm just an average 'Joe'?"

In a world of nearly unlimited possibilities and possible stories you could tell yourself about yourself, you have chosen "I'm a normal 'Joe'" as an identity script?

Is that an identity that'll inspire you to jump out of bed each morning to cultivate new habits and skills?

It may be a safe, easy, comfortable identity, yet it's hardly inspiring.

Anais Nin, the French-born American essayist, assured us that "Life shrinks or expands according to one's courage."

The greater the vision and personal quest, the greater the courage required, and most certainly, the greater the resistance – the headwinds you'll experience.

Do you think Ben thought of himself as a normal, average "Joe," or did he aspire to a greater ideal and vision for himself?

By identifying his 13 Virtues – the character he wanted to cultivate in the future – Ben challenged himself to refine his habits.

I can hear someone saying, "I don't need to improve anything. I'm perfect just how I am!"

Sure, you are.

And, if you don't like the results you're experiencing, feel free to say this aloud:

I am perfect, AND I could use some work.

Are you exploring?
Are you documenting?
Are you challenging yourself?

Are you the F*cking captain of your ship or a passenger along for some joy ride?

I saw this on social media a while back, and it broke my heart: "This isn't the life I was looking for."

"Not the life you're looking for?" I get it; sometimes, really bad sh*t happens. However, are you looking for a life or creating one?

Let's follow his logic, "Oh! There it is! I've found it! That's it! It's over here – the life I've been looking for. I was looking in the wrong place. I can't believe it was hiding over there!"

The truth is, our words reflect the quality of our thoughts and certainly the stories we're telling ourselves. "This isn't the life I was looking for"? That is hardly Invictus material.[36]

Such language suggests life is a passive event, something that happens to us, where we have little or no influence over our conditions and outcomes.

One more time, everyone together this time: It's both!

We can affect our outcomes, *and* life "happens to us."

I wish life were just a joy ride. Wouldn't it be nice if we could coast *all* the time? "The interesting thing about coasting," Brian Tracy likes to say, "is you can only do it in one direction."

When you decide to captain your life, you become responsible for *all* of it.

The irony is that when you grab the helm, take ownership – *begin steering your stories with purpose and intention* – the journey becomes far more enjoyable.

---

[36] See the *Invictus* poem at the end of the book.

MASTERY (REVISITER)

Beginner's Mind

初心

*"No man is free who cannot
command himself."*
~Pythagoras

We'd traveled nearly 40 hours just to get to our boat,
The Indies Trader III, a surf charter. An 88-foot yacht was
waiting to take us around the Mentawai islands to hunt for
great surf.

Once aboard, we cruised overnight to our first surf spot.
As dawn broke, it quickly became evident the surf was

small. Nonetheless, all seven of us eagerly unpacked our boards and began prepping, putting on the fins, waxing up, and attaching our leashes. Leashes are rubber ropes connected to your ankle; they're designed to keep your surfboard close (within about six feet), so if you fall off your board, you can quickly retrieve it.

In Indonesia, most of the waves break over coral reefs. The bottom of the ocean contours the waves, making them look remarkably beautiful. The reefs also create hollow surf, allowing more experienced riders to slide under the curl and into the "tube." Tube riding is one of the most incredible sensations imaginable; surfers will travel the world for the experience.

Eager to get out of the 90-plus-degree heat and into the ocean, we all jumped right in. After a few rides, I sat on my board, awaiting the next set.

Suddenly, I felt a tug on my right leg. As the wave approached, the tug became more intense. Instantly, I was pulled under the passing wave. As I surfaced, I quickly realized that my leash had tangled around a coral head.

Still stuck, another wave followed closely. I was pulled under again! This time, upon surfacing, I looked at my buddy, who had no idea what was happening. I shouted, "My f*cking leash is stuck!" Then another wave, and under I went for the third time! The situation rapidly went from slightly comical to "Holy sh*t, this is getting dangerous!"

On the one hand, I knew that all I needed to do was remove my leash, and I'd be safe and free – simple enough.

Yet, because the leash was brand new, I was unfamiliar with it and couldn't for the life of me (pun intended) find where the end was hiding so I could strip it off my ankle, despite several attempts. No matter how desperately I searched, using my hands to feel around my ankle, the end of the leash was nowhere to be found. The leash's Velcro was so tightly entwined that its end was indistinguishable. Even worse, the more I struggled, the harder it was to find.

Another wave came. I was pulled under again! My mind started spinning.

STORIES!

Just two stories, actually.

The first story: Holy sh*t! So, this is how it goes down? You surf for nearly 40 years, and you're gonna drown stuck to a coral head – on your very first f*cking session in Indo!!!

Fortunately, the other story was a bit more hopeful and optimistic. Relax! All you have to do is find the end of the leash. **Relax!** Hold your breath, and just repeat. You can do this as long as needed until you get this f*cking leash off!

A few seconds later, I found the end of the leash. That was that. Embarrassing, yes. Fatal, no.

All told, it was approximately 90 seconds of drama that felt like a lifetime.

I share this story because of its lesson – one that took me a few days to grasp.

I'd jumped into the ocean with a great deal of confidence and certainly some ego. It was time to start "ripping" up the waves! Unfortunately, and nearly tragically, I possessed little respect for the ocean, the new environment, and perhaps most of all, my new equipment. My only consideration was, "It's small. It's shallow. Let's see if we can have some fun, and, oh yeah, try not to hit the reef!"

In short, had I just paused and slowed down, the entire situation could have been avoided.

The moral of the story: Approaching situations, both old and new, with greater awareness and a beginner's mind, can yield untold rewards; **it may even save your life**.

Speaking of "beginner's mind," I'm compelled to share the "bad news" I promised in the previous chapter. It's *why* most people won't track their habits, despite knowing that habit tracking will aid them in their efforts to get wherever they want to go.

Crazy, I know!

It turns out there is a force so maniacal, strong, and powerful that it works every moment to thwart your efforts.

By the way, that is *not* hyperbole.

Each and every moment, this force works *against* you until it begins to work *for* you! This force also will make your journey seem impossible *at first*.

This force is often misrepresented as "the resistance." Sigmund Freud referenced this term to address the ego's unwillingness to uncover repressed information (stories)

most often rooted in the emotion of *fear*, as in fearing a
story might unearth a way *forward*, presenting growth and
challenges.

"Courage," John Wayne advised, "is being scared to
death and saddling up anyway." It turns out that the
definitive quality behind "the resistance" is *not* actually fear
or any other negative emotion.

While many in psychology and coaching circles
admonish negative emotions as worthless, it seems evident
they serve a purpose. For instance, fear and many other
negative emotions can provide potentially valuable, even
life-saving guidance, particularly when backed by the
aforementioned special ingredient.

Yes, here it is again: **Awareness**.

Negative emotions, including fear, doubt, anger, and
jealousy, are inescapable. It's essential to understand *how* to
manage them and extract their vital, helpful information
while discarding the rest.

Awareness allows us to "elevate" and observe our
negative emotions – to step outside and beyond the
Behavior Echo-System. Awareness lets us ask with curiosity
and resourcefulness: "How can I use this negative emotion
constructively? How can I learn from this feeling? Is there a
lesson here? Is there a way this emotion can help move me
closer to my goals?

Document your feelings when you notice them.

Recall the Depressed, Failure, and Hope chapters. Each was riddled with negative emotions and, not coincidentally, corresponding life lessons to help one move forward positively.

Incredibly, some studies cite the psychological, emotional, and physiological benefits of narrative – writing about our disappointments, "failures," disheartening events, and even traumas to better process them. One such study is titled: *"Forming a story: the health benefits of narrative."*[42]

Recall, near the end of the *Failure* chapter, I commented, "there is even more to the story." This is it!

By writing about, recounting, and facing our "failures," we begin to better process the experience and understand it as a past event. We can even begin to detach and learn from the experience and then let it go.

If "the resistance" isn't fear or another negative emotion, what is it?

Here are a few more clues: This force is invisible, and it's why everyone sometimes feels "stuck" or like they aren't tapping into their potential.

Battling back "the resistance" is your Gettysburg, Normandie, Yorktown, and Waterloo.

It's you vs. the resistance.

The good news is that the battle is winnable!
The other news is that it will be difficult before it's easy.

The resistance is so powerful that authors, philosophers, and the greatest thinkers since time immemorial spoke about its challenges. Please consider the following:

"It is *notorious* how powerful is the force of habit."
~Charles Darwin

"Habits are cobwebs at first and cables at last."
~Chinese proverb.

"Habit is the most imperious of all masters."
~Johann Wolfgang Von Goethe

"The chains of habit are too weak to be felt until they are too strong to be broken."
~Samuel Johnson

To be clear: Habit is the resistance. It operates at every "level" in the 3 Circles of Behavior Echo-System.

everythingastory.com

Ironically, the very same force that binds you can set you free! Hence, perhaps my favorite habit quote of all by Ambrose Bierce, an American journalist, poet, and short story writer:

"Habit, n.: A shackle for the free."

You are *free* to establish *any* habit you choose. Beware, though: The ones you develop will shackle you.
Choose wisely!

So, if habit becomes fixed and binds us at every level within the 3 Circles of Behavior Echo-System, how can we apply the same force to set ourselves free?

Drum roll, please...*Practice!*
By taking command of our habits via habit tracking.
That is all there is to it.
Simple and difficult, at first.

Difficult because your existing habits will oppose your efforts every step of the way.

Now, you may be thinking:

A) I've had it with the word "habit"! I thought this was about story and thinking![37]

B) Or: There's no way personal mastery is as simple as daily habit tracking! (Despite my sharing that this is precisely what monks and priests do to refine their behaviors and thoughts!)

C) Or: This is going to take way too much time. I need something that will work now! A quick fix!

D) Or: There's no way tracking a few simple habits for 28 days (four weeks, following P.A.R.R.) will help me. I need BIG things to happen.

E) Or you may be saying all the above!

If this is what you're thinking, TERRIFIC!

It's important to remember that ALL great things begin small. As Lao Tzu put it, "The longest journey begins with a single step."

One good habit tends to lead to another. One good decision tends to lead to another.

By putting your attention and focus on just one habit for 28 days (four weeks), a few fantastic things happen:

1. You'll understand and respect the **force of habit** and the challenge involved with honoring your plan and intention.

---

[37] It's about story, thinking, and much more. The force of habit influences our repeated thoughts, stories, and behaviors.

2. As a byproduct of mindful tracking – adhering to your plan – you'll improve and strengthen your **discipline**.
3. You'll demonstrate **self-efficacy**, which is simply the ability to produce a desired result. This will make you feel happier, increase your self-esteem, and demonstrate that you have control, which will provide momentum! The opposite is true, of course. If you establish a plan and do not honor it, you won't feel so great.[43]

Thus, it's imperative you start small, with just one habit, ideally. This sets you up to win the day! The P.A.R.R. method, by design, teaches you how to set up small, initial "targets."

***

So, yes, taking command of your habits takes a lot of time – a lifetime!

Yet, what is a lifetime, *really*?

Isn't a "lifetime" experienced just one day at a time?

Can you track for just one day?

The answer is you absolutely can!

If I offered you $1,000 to track just three habits tomorrow, I can virtually guarantee that you would have no problem doing so, presuming $1,000 was a meaningful sum of money – a motivating force.

Since you can track for one day, you can most certainly do it again the next day, and the next.

What worthwhile captain isn't *committed* to arriving at their destination? Isn't it every captain's *responsibility* and *duty* to arrive successfully?

KEEPING YOUR HANDS ON THE HELM, most of the time, IS THE ESSENCE OF PERSONAL MASTERY.

Daily habit tracking, journaling, and script reviews help assure that your hands are on the helm. It's also how you will know if you're steering your thoughts and behaviors toward your ideal destination.

Here's a quick script – a mantra. Feel free to say it aloud: *I am the captain! I'm in command of my thoughts and behaviors NOW. (Repeat)*

PERSONAL MASTERY IS A ONE-DAY-AT-A-TIME PHENOMENON.

This leads me to a somewhat magical observation about learning Zen. You might even consider it a Zen koan:

"Learning Zen is a phenomenon of gold and dung. Before you understand it, it's gold. After you understand it, it's dung."

The same can be said for personal mastery.

Before you learn it, it's gold. It's something everyone thinks is special, maybe even unattainable. Yet, once they understand it, it is pure DUNG!

Personal mastery, much like the learning of Zen, has almost nothing to do with ideas and everything to do with *practice!*

If you read this entire book (just a collection of ideas) and never apply them – it's really just a pile of horsesh*t.

I hate to say it, given the time and energy that went into writing it, but it's true. It may as well be firewood.

This is precisely *why* each book in this trilogy (*The Habit Factor*, *The Pressure Paradox*, and *Everything*) has an "Application" section. It's also part of why The Habit Factor app was released *before* the book!

By commanding the helm, guiding your most important, personal narratives and behaviors intentionally (most of the time) toward your goals and ideals, you *must* move closer to them![38]

This daily practice doesn't make anyone perfect; it just makes them BETTER.

---

[38] Unless the environment is overpowering; see the "Three Circles" chapter.

While I wish there were a "secret" or something extremely exciting and sexy – a quick fix, a microwave solution, ready in a minute – it doesn't exist. Even *The Secret* itself (referring to the popular book and movie) doesn't work without the force of habit! Hence, The Habit Factor.

If you are looking for a secret, this is it!

Personal mastery isn't quick or pretty; it requires discipline. The good news is that discipline is a *habit* that is cultivated and strengthened each time you practice habit tracking.

Thus, when you are tracking, you are on the path – you're "on track."

You'll know for certain you're on the path toward personal mastery when you begin to enjoy the slow, difficult, and ordinary more than the quick, easy, and seductive.

The great news is, once you're tracking and on the path, you'll compile one successful day after another, *most of the time*. The compilation – the compounding effect – of mostly successful days is what results in a lifetime of beautiful results.

Are you on the path?

Is today just another day? Or is it Day One?

You decide.

INDICATORS

"The purpose of life is not to be happy. It is to be useful, to be honorable, to be compassionate, to have it make some difference that you have lived and lived well."
~Ralph Waldo Emerson

"Your purpose in life is to find your purpose and give your whole heart and soul to it."
~Buddha

Surfers are peculiar. They have a lingo – a language all their own. Growing up, it was captivating.

Surf spots are designated as either reef, point, or beach breaks. When it comes to waves, there are lefts, rights, A-frames, tubes, barrels, and shacks. The surf can be hollow or fat, and surfing maneuvers have funny names like cutbacks, hanging five, off the lips, 360s, and aerials. Timing your surf sessions is essential; one of the classic lines in surf culture is, "You should have been here yesterday."

The ocean can be "blown out" or "glassy." It might be high tide or low tide. There are unfavorable labels like "kook" and "barney."

The slang is endless: sick, epic, maxed out, back door, guns, dropping in, onshore, offshore, twin, quad, tri, rocker, wipeouts, victory at sea, morning sickness, bailing, caught inside, impact zone, whitewater, gnarly, and more.

Oh yeah – there's also a whole lot of "bro," "dude," and "stoked."

All of it was enthralling as a teen. Today, it's mostly fodder for social media.

The greatest value of all of it isn't the language or even the culture; it's the association with mother nature and the ocean. Her lessons abound, particularly when it comes to *reading* our environment – recognizing the signs, clues, and signals about what might lie ahead.[39]

---

[39] See *The Pressure Paradox* "Mastery" chapter for more lessons learned from water. In the Acknowledgments of *The Habit Factor*, I first thank the ocean.

INDICATORS

In pursuit of perpetual stoke, surfers chase swells all over the world. Thanks to the internet and modern forecasting technologies, it's not uncommon for top pros to drop everything and fly halfway around the world for the right swell. Typically, locals have a few "go-to" spots to check for the best surf on any given day.

Surfing can be so addictive that labels like "surf bum" exist. Many surfers will go out of their way to craft a lifestyle around their passion. They'll prioritize *where* they live above even where they'll work or how they'll make money. Fabricated or not, the "Not When the Surf's Up Construction Company" exemplifies the sentiment perfectly.

One surf term has been calling my attention lately: **indicators.**

A point break is a surf spot where the land jettisons out into the ocean and sharply curves back. The "point" is where the land pushes out. It creates a beautiful wrapping effect as waves sweep past, extending waves and, depending on the break, creating rides that can last minutes.[44]

Waves arrive in bunches called "sets." There's a period of calm between sets known as "lulls." Lulls are sometimes as short as a few minutes or as long as 15-plus minutes.

Nearly every point break has an *indicator* – a spot beyond the actual surf spot. Indicators are only noticed when a surfer elevates their gaze. By altering their perspective beyond their current situation, they get a glimpse into the future and see waves (and possible rides) coming their way.

In life, indicators are different. They're a beautiful blend of our past experiences (values, strengths, weaknesses, affinities, passions) coupled with our current cues (friends, family, occupation, problems, opportunities, and even random events); Collectively, they reveal what may lie ahead.

The world's first adventurers set sail across open oceans, relying on the North Star as a trustworthy beacon. The North Star guided sailors toward their ideal destination.

Polaris, the North Star's official name, is located almost directly above the North Pole, a position that never changes in the sky.

Just like great past explorers, we must know our North Star – the values we hold most dear, the ones that will guide us. And, like Polaris, it's helpful to have one foremost value that never changes.[40]

For the most part, values guide our behaviors and actions from one moment to the next. When we fully subscribe to them, values are deep-seated beliefs bolstered by stories that justify those values. Our core values help to solidify our self-construct – our identity.[41]

Values are so essential that the world's greatest organizations and companies will take months, possibly years, to ensure their core values are accurate. Some companies may call these "precepts" or even "guiding

---

[40] A terrific exercise for this is coming next!
[41] Values exercise forthcoming.

principles." Either way, they're designed to guide the entire organization's behaviors – to ensure everyone rows in the same direction.

By tallying our life's indicators and overlaying them with the daily *art of practice* – habit tracking, meditation, journaling, and script management – something magical emerges. [42]

The Path!

Following presentations, courses, workshops, and even webinars, I'll field comments like, "I'm just not sure what my big goal should be." Or, "I don't really know what my purpose is." Or, "I'm not sure what I should be doing with my life."

These "lost" type comments sound nearly identical. My response is typically the same:

You do know. And, you do not know.

A paradoxical and simple truth.

From the earliest chapters, I've promoted a simple, succinct definition of success: "Creating your ideal future." That is the great quest. Or, as Oprah Winfrey put it, "One's greatest adventure is to live the life of their dreams."

---

[42] Script management is a compilation of script refinement, edits, and programming; more on this later.

Such a journey is both an inward and outward exploration.

We must put in time and effort to identify our ideal future, character (identity), goals, and ideals. We also must look inward to assess our strengths, weaknesses, stories, and all the related habitual programming.

Chances are excellent that with ample reflection, guided by essential questions (aided by stillness, solitude, and silence), we'll notice life's indicators guiding us toward the PATH – our purpose.

And, as anyone who proceeds down any path will tell you, ultimately, the path *shifts.*

Change is a great constant in life.
A superb example of a simple, paradoxical truth.

Someone may feel deeply that their purpose is to be a good parent. Still, they'll wake up one day – if they're lucky – with the day-to-day responsibilities of *that* purpose in their rearview mirror.

They may wonder, "Now, what?"

In my teens, I thought my purpose was to be an artist and art director.[43] In my 20s, I was confident it was to be an

---

[43] I mention a painting I sold after cleaning out my storage unit in the Acknowledgments.

entrepreneur and teacher. In my 30s, it was evident that my purpose was to be an entrepreneur, serving the community and developing and coaching employees. In my 40s, I knew I was to become an author and teacher – a specialist in the subject matter of HABIT.

Now, after years of teaching, coaching, and having authored a few books, I believe I'm a guide, teacher, coach, and forever student. Yet, despite this "belief," I'm completely open to *indicators* that could lead me in a half-dozen unforeseeable directions.

The beauty is that all these paths reveal a shared pattern:
1) We must venture down *a path*.
2) The path invariably changes.
3) We must adjust course.
4) Clues present themselves as key *indicators*.
5) Our core values and North Star serve as crucial guides.
6) The noble path is always underscored by SERVICE.

Here are a couple exercises from our <u>Automatic Goals</u> course to help anyone find their purpose.

> "You can't go back and change the beginning, but you can start where you are and change the ending."
> - *C.S. Lewis*

Completed? ☐   *Grade your effort! (1 - 5):*   *Date:*

VALUES DEATH MATCH

Values guide our behavior and decision-making. Becoming acutely aware of your TOP values is powerful.
Take the challenge. Do your best to determine your #1 value!

N

thehabitfactor.com
© Equilibrium Enterprises, Inc.

everythingastory.com   The Habit Factor®

45

"You can't go back and change the beginning, but you can start where you are and change the ending."

- C.S. Lewis

Completed? ☐   *Grade your effort! (1 - 5):*   *Date:*

INDICATORS/PURPOSE

Value can be found at the intersection of your natural affinities, knowledge, skills, passions, and interests – where they all overlap to solve a problem.

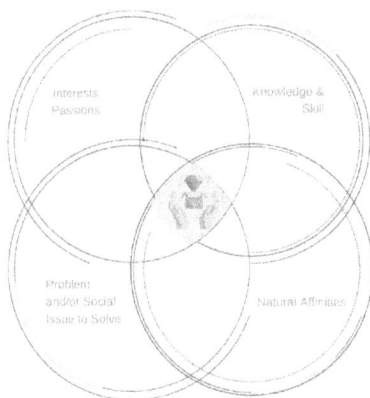

The idea behind the exercises is that our greatest value is to be of service to others.

Do you recall Campbell's Hero's Journey and the cycle from the "Meaning" chapter? Each hero begins their journey as a solo affair – it's all about *me*.

Why can't I figure out MY purpose!?
Why does nobody understand ME!?
Why does nobody listen to ME!?
Why do I have no friends!?
Why is MY life so f*cked up!?
#FML
Me, Me, Me.

If you saw *Star Wars*, you may recall Luke being a whiny little b*tch upon arriving at his Uncle Ben's farm.

At the starting point of every Hero's Journey, they're a whiny little b*tch – one who *habitually* complains, blames, and shames others and, interestingly, themselves.

They're so myopic – so focused on *themselves* and their problems – that they can't see the inescapable truth:

The best way to help themselves is to begin helping others.

At a certain point, with some good fortune (that typically arrives disguised as an unavoidable problem), a shift happens. They notice that their self-centered #FML mentality isn't serving them.

So, they begin asking questions.
The better the questions, the better the answers.

How can I create value?
How can I be of service?
What am I naturally good at?
What do my friends say I'm great at?
What skills and habits would make me more valuable?
What gifts do I have that I can share with the world?
How can my passions, skills, and talents help to serve others?

Einstein put it this way: "Do not try to become a person of success, but rather try to become a person of value."

Like happiness, success is the result of indirect and direct efforts.

The *direct* effort is stepping onto the Path, moving toward an ideal destination, and tracking.
The *indirect* effort is serving others.

At 15, I spent about four weeks at Catalina Island Camps. There I met Felipe – a lifelong dear friend.
Catalina Island Camps separated the boys' and girls' camps. Each respective camp was further divided (today, it might be called "gamified") into "Yale" and "Princeton" for the boys and "Wellesley" and "Radcliffe" for the girls.
The campers and counselors would compete, tallying up points in various competitions. At the beginning of each camp session, there was a vote for each team's captain.

Typically, the older "senior" campers – the 15-year-olds –
can run for captain.

I wasn't just encouraged to run; I was assured I'd win.

At the last minute, I heard Felipe was running for
captain. There may have been other candidates; I can't
recall. With little warning, we were told we'd have to give a
brief speech about why we wanted to be captain. I went
first, unprepared and ambivalent; it was bland, at best.

Then my buddy Felipe stood before everyone. Felipe
grew up in Mexico City. His family relocated from Germany
after World War II. Felipe was tan with light blond hair and
hazel eyes. At 15, he was already a world-class sailor who'd
represented Mexico in a recent world championship.

Felipe began speaking quietly and humbly – a welcome
contradiction to what I presented, I'm sure. Further, Felipe
possessed a beautiful, charismatic Spanish accent. His
speech was succinct and superior. It was over in a few
minutes and culminated with the following sentences:

"*I theeenk we shaaalllll whheeeiiiin.*"

"*I know wheeeee wheeeeeeeeeeelll wheeeeeeeeiiiiiiinn!!!*"

With that, the entire Princeton contingent – 100-plus
campers and counselors – began cheering, jumping up and
down, chanting, "Felipe!" "Felipe!" "Felipe!"

That was it. Felipe was the Princeton captain.

I tucked my tail between my legs, congratulated my
buddy, and laughed.

Here's a related story – one I'm sure my brother Rich
will thank me for later:

Two years after Felipe's spectacular victory campaign, it was my younger brother Richard's turn to run for Princeton captain. That year, I returned as a sailing instructor (thanks to Felipe).

Richard not only ran for captain, but he won*!*

The established ritual for the newly appointed captain is to lead their team in a cheer for the opposing team as a sign of good sportsmanship. In this case, it was Yale.

The entire Princeton team gathered around Rich – a massive huddle formed on the field. About 100-plus campers and a dozen or so counselors all put their hands into the center of a massive pile of bodies.

Rich began the cheer, spelling out the opposition's name, Y-A-L-E.

"Give me a Y!" The collective shouted back, "Y!"

"Give me an A!" The crowd yelled back, "A!"

"Give me an L!" "L!" reverberated across the camp's cove.

Undoubtedly consumed by the excitement, lost in the moment, Rich concluded his cheer right there.

"What's that spell!?" He screamed.

A few campers looked around, and there was an awkward silence. Then a few people quizzically muttered, "*YAL???*"

Chaos and hilarity ensued.

#truestory

Of course, Rich went on to become a great captain, a legendary camper, and ultimately a great counselor for years to come![44]

While those may be the most comical camp stories I can actually share, Felipe is also behind one of the most profound stories (soon to follow).

***

In the "Mastery" chapter, we reviewed a crucial concept: The Force of Habit is the one force that binds everyone:

The first essential and unavoidable truth is that **energy is naturally efficient**. Energy seeks a path of least resistance. Think of water's tendency to flow to low points. Energy also tends to organize itself into patterns and rhythms. Consider waves, including sound waves, ocean waves, and light waves. Nature is a beautiful exhibition of pattern and rhythm: high-tide, low-tide, the weather, and seasons (winter, summer, spring, autumn).

The second unavoidable truth is that **you are energy**. Thus, your patterns are rhythms (habits) formed either with your guidance or without it.

Awareness is required to identify your goals and ideals and the habits that will help you achieve them.

---

[44] You might recognize Rich from the *3 C's of Succcess*. Also, the best brother anyone could ask for.

Both habit and awareness are necessary. Both are important.

If you had to be mindful 24/7, you'd collapse rather quickly. Awareness makes you the programmer. Your programs are the habits you craft.

Habit and awareness complement each other.

@thehabitfactor

everythingastory.com

The third unavoidable truth is that your goals and ideals will require energy to "arrive."

By establishing habits aligned with your goals and ideals, you position yourself to arrive more effectively and efficiently. [45] Habit is the most efficient and effective use of behavior energy.

---

[45] Habit Alignment technology™ introduced in 2009 with the app.

However, just like the wind, habit can be destructive, or it can be helpful and propel us toward our ideal destination. It depends.

Most often, it depends on the skill of the captain. There's a great adage: "Smooth seas do not make for a skillful sailor." The same can be said for life. It's the adventurers, explorers, and "failures" who, coupled with a fair amount of reflection, become skillful with years of experience and "failure" behind them.

Is the captain able to read the indicators? Can they amalgamate their life experiences and extract their crucial lessons? Are they committed to arriving successfully at their ideal destination? Do they know how to harness the force of the wind favorably and how to trim the sails as necessary? Are they commanding the helm most of the time?

***

That summer, Felipe offered to teach me to sail. To this day, I absolutely love sailing, and I owe that distinction to him.

As a world-class competitive sailor, Felipe taught me many sailing nuances.

"*Look,*" Felipe shouted, pointing into the distance. We were sailing just inside the camp's cove. Felipe held the tiller (a small boat's steering wheel – its helm) as he guided our little 14-foot Capri sailboat. He was pointing to an area in the distance. "Do you see it?"

At the same time, he asked me to grab the tiller, so we switched positions. I was now steering our tiny sailboat.

"What? Where?" I couldn't figure out what he was pointing to. I was looking for something solid – something tangible.

"There!" Felipe pressed, pointing with intensity. "Look over there! It's much stronger over there!"

About 200 yards in the distance, near a point just off the rocks, I finally saw what Felipe was pointing at. A rippling current was noticeable on the ocean's surface – a strong indicator. It was the wind!

Felipe directed me to steer straight for it.

As we approached the area, the wind captured our sails, our boat tipped to its side – it was "heeling."

We began to fly.

Goal Complete!

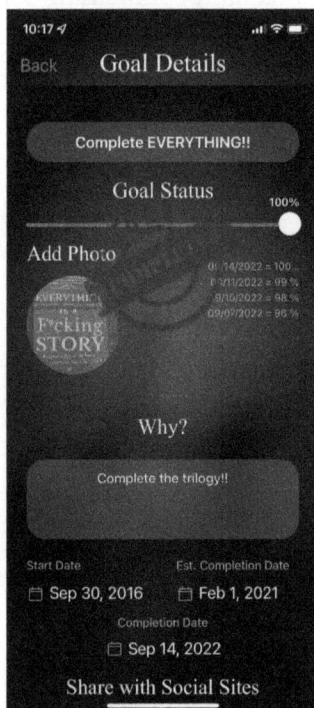

Screenshot: The Habit Factor app.

Each book in the "trilogy" was *tracked* and completed using The Habit Factor. ®

PRACTICE & EXERCISES

"Vision without action is a daydream.
Action without vision is a nightmare."
~ Japanese proverb

"All life is an experiment, the more
experiments you make the better."
~Ralph W. Emerson

Experiment! Explore! Practice! And, please, track your f*cking habits! Start journaling, manage your scripts! (More days than not...) Make this not dung!

**Grab the
F*cking HELM
Captain!**

Live your greatest adventure!

everythingastory.com

Who? Beliefs Values Meaning How?
What? Where? Purpose Why? When?

Past | Present | Future

STORIES

~FACT & FICTION~

Everything!

everythingastory.com

"You can't go back and change the beginning, but you can start where you are and change the ending."

~ *C.S. Lewis*

Completed? ☐   *Grade your effort! (1 - 5):*   *Date:*

THE ULTIMATE END STORY

Obituary: Nothing Changes

You are reflecting on your life as if you are a third-party observer. Who was this person? Who did they most impact and love? What were they passionate about? What will they be most remembered for? What key accomplishments and achievements were they most proud of?

When done with conviction, this can be the ultimate lever – the ultimate PAIN (regret story) that compels a new identity and related behavior changes!

everythingastory.com

The Habit Factor®

> **"You can't go back and change the beginning, but you can start where you are and change the ending."**
>
> *- C.S. Lewis*

Completed? ☐ *Grade your effort! (1 - 5):* *Date:*

THE ULTIMATE END STORY
Obituary: Ideal End Story

You are reflecting on your life as if you are a third-party observer. Who was this person? Who did they most impact and love? What were they passionate about? What will they be most remembered for? What key accomplishments and achievements were they most proud of?

> "You can't go back and change the beginning, but you
> can start where you are and change the ending."
>
> ~ *C.S. Lewis*

Completed? ☐   *Grade your effort! (1 - 5):*   *Date:*

THE BUCKET LIST
Get on track!

One life to live. Consider ALL the achievements and experiences you MUST have before you die. This should excite you and fire you up! They are absolutely possible! Examples: visit Yellowstone National Park with family, skydive, learn to speak Spanish, learn to play piano, etc.

Learning/Skills	Experiences	Travel

everythingastory.com

The Habit Factor®

"You can't go back and change the beginning, but you can start where you are and change the ending."

- C.S. Lewis

Completed? ☐   *Grade your effort! (1 - 5):*   *Date:*

BALANCE WHEEL

Balance is not just a moment in time. It's a dynamic process of adjustment. Knowing this, it's wise to periodically assess our critical wellness areas to identify WHERE we should direct our energy and attention to find balance.

Foundation

everythingastory.com

The Habit Factor®

Categories: Mind, Body, Social, Spiritual, Financial, Professional, Adventure/Lifestyle, Emotional

"You can't go back and change the beginning, but you can start where you are and change the ending."

~ C.S. Lewis

Completed? ☐   *Grade your effort! (1 - 5)*:   *Date*:

SCRIPT MANAGEMENT

Review and manage the related scripts for the stories that
"Really Freakin' Matter," beginning with:

WHO?

Who are you?
For each of the roles you play, there are related storylines and scripts.
For instance: Parent, Spouse, Sibling, Occupation

I AM... a supportive, loving parent who makes time to listen intently

Role:
I AM...
I AM...

Role:
I AM...
I AM...

Role:
I AM...
I AM...

Role:
I AM...
I AM...

Now, write the meaningful, supportive WHY story.

Remember, ALL storylines and scripts must pass the H.E.R.O. checklist.
Is it Hopeful, Empowering, Responsible, and Optimistic?
Ideal characters and roles influence ideal behaviors, habits, and skills!

everythingastory.com

"You can't go back and change the beginning, but you can start where you are and change the ending."

~ C.S. Lewis

Completed? ☐   *Grade your effort! (1 - 5):*   *Date:*

SCRIPT MANAGEMENT

Review and manage the related scripts for the stories that
"Really Freakin' Matter."

WHAT?

What are you passionately interested in becoming?
What are you passionately interested in achieving and experiencing in your life?

I am becoming a great... author, painter, lawyer

I am becoming...

I am becoming...

I intend to create...

I intend to create...

I will experience...

I will experience...

Now, write the meaningful, supportive WHY story.

Remember, ALL storylines and scripts must pass the H.E.R.O. checklist.
Is it Hopeful, Empowering, Responsible, and Optimistic?

everythingastory.com

> "You can't go back and change the beginning, but you can start where you are and change the ending."
>
> ~ *C.S. Lewis*

Completed? ☐   *Grade your effort! (1 - 5):*   *Date:*

SCRIPT MANAGEMENT

Review and manage the related scripts for the stories that
"Really Freakin' Matter."

WHERE (Disposition)

Where are you currently emotionally anchored, most of the time?
What is your default disposition? Happy, harmonious, kind, easygoing? Or,
disgruntled, angry, frustrated, disappointed, and sad?

My current emotional anchor/disposition is...

Where would you prefer to be emotionally anchored (if different)?

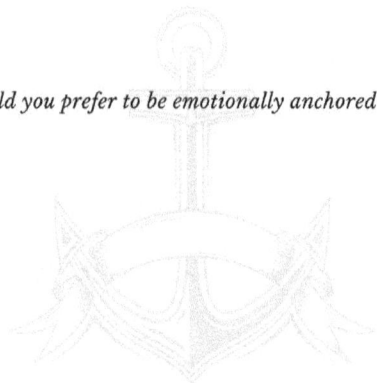

Is it Hopeful, Empowering, Responsible, and Optimistic?

everythingastory.com

> **"You can't go back and change the beginning, but you can start where you are and change the ending."**
>
> *- C.S. Lewis*

Completed? ☐ *Grade your effort! (1 - 5):* *Date:*

SCRIPT MANAGEMENT
What stories are in your gunnysack?

What stories are weighing you down? Are there any stories in the gunnysack that you can discard? Which ones have taught you the greatest lessons?

The stories in my gunnysack holding me back are:

The negative emotions these stories bring include:

For example, jealousy, disappointment, anger, frustration, shame, guilt

The lessons I've learned from these experiences are:

The Exercises

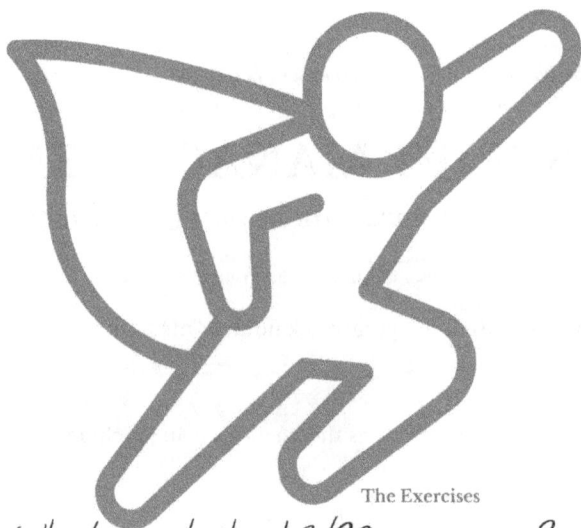

Who else can be the HERO of your story?

H.E.R.O.

Scripts & Storylines worthy of a Hero's Journey

Imagination!

Backed by sincere desire.

everythingastory.com

QUESTIONS AND ANSWERS

1) **Why do you write about habits and skills almost interchangeably, and why do they share the same space in the behavior echo-system?**

   When it comes to habits and skills, their similarities far outweigh their differences, which are mostly semantic. As each develops, they follow a similar path relative to the "wiring" in the brain. At the highest competence level, the similarities are striking. To learn more, look up the "4 Stages of competence."[46] Additionally, check out the Habits 2 Goals podcast episodes Habits vs. Skills and Habits vs. Skills: What's the Difference?

2) **What is the voice in my head?**

   The dominant voice is often labeled the "critic" due to the habit of critiquing others, events, experiences, and, most often, ourselves. The more we refrain from habitually judging others, the less likely we'll be to criticize ourselves.

   The voice may also be described as your consciousness, trained by a lifetime of unconscious reinforcement and practice – habitual use.

3) **How can I stop the voice in my head? The chatter and stories never seem to end.**

   Instead of viewing the voice as something to stop, view it as an ally, coach, encourager, and friend. While it's near impossible to stop the voice, it *is* possible to calm, quiet, redirect, and control it – most of the time.

   The objective is to command and control the stories you hear – steering, harnessing, and redirecting them.

   When you recognize the stories and voices as distinctly separate from yourself:

- You become the observer, not what is observed. This perspective makes the stories and voices easier to control, steer, and direct.
- You naturally *distance* yourself from past critical stories and events and can better appreciate the lessons.
- You're able to conduct role play and imagination exercises. For example, what would [respected person] do in this situation?

4) What is the best way to meditate if I've never had success meditating?

Meditation's great misunderstanding is thinking the objective is to arrive at no thought. The moment you realize you've arrived at "no thought," you have a thought – you're thinking! Many people don't realize that meditation is a period to reflect, appreciate, set intentions, and plan. It's not just an exercise for mindfulness in the moment.

From my experience, meditation's great value isn't *stopping* internal stories and voices. Instead, it's noticing them, assessing their value, and then discarding, replacing, or redirecting what's unhelpful. The beauty is, you can step outside your behavior echo-system and observe your feelings, emotions, behaviors, and environment any time when you meditate. You can also assess if they're in alignment with your goals and ideals.

When meditating, consider the following:

- Keep a pad and pencil with you as you meditate to help you clear your mind and capture your thoughts, typically in the form of to-do items. Freeing your mind of urgent tasks creates relaxation and makes it easier to control and direct your attention. David Allen, author of *Getting Things Done*, observed, "The mind is meant for creating ideas, not holding them."
- Use the 6 Stories that Really Frickin' matter as a guided meditation. Go through each script as you meditate: Who,

What, Where, Why, When, and How. Notice your feelings, reflect on their underlying stories, and question the accuracy of those storylines. Consider alternative, more favorable scripts and alternate guided meditations that direct your mind favorably.

- Use meditation as a practice to guide attention toward feelings and emotions of love, kindness, gratitude, and appreciation.[46]

5) Much of this seems like Pollyanna thinking. There are real events, and you can't just make up airy-fairy thinking to make bad things disappear!

You are correct. Real events exist. At the same time, future storylines are undetermined. No one knows how any story ends. It's only Pollyanna thinking if you discredit the facts.

Recall the "Hope" chapter: Jimmy's new, exciting venture fell through, and he assessed his situation. It was true that he was low on funds. But it was *not* true that he would be living out of his car. Jimmy promoted a fear-based storyline that never came to pass.

The future holds a spectrum of possibilities. Hopeful stories offer tremendous support for those in crises and challenging circumstances. Challenging times may also dredge up a lifetime of stored negative stories that may lead us astray if we forecast and steer toward them.

The truth is that it can be helpful to *anticipate* (rather than dwell upon) potential unfavorable events (the opposite of Pollyanna thinking) to plan, prepare and, when necessary, practice to help

---

[46] Learn more about meditation at https://everythingastory.com and see the ancillary Meditation and Mantra guide.

ensure a more favorable outcome is realized.[47] At the same time, you can idealize future storylines to create an intention – a direction – fueling hope and possibilities.

6) **I keep thinking about a fight with my spouse (best friend, boss, lover, etc.). No matter what I do, it keeps replaying in my head. It's made me sick.**
Emotions and feelings affect and guide our focus and attention. An emotionally charged event will continue to "play" and repeat itself, and you'll continually rehash things you should have said and done.

Changing your immediate environment helps control and refocus your attention – the more immersive, the better. It's hard to feel down when you're scuba diving, riding a bike, jogging, visiting friends, etc.

With the power of reflection and distance, you can observe the story from another perspective – the other party or a neutral third party. Consider that your truth is just one interpretation of the story. As your awareness grows, you may find common ground. Extract the event's lessons by asking, "How can I use this?" and "How can I learn from this going forward?"

7) **I like the simplicity of the 3 Circles behavior model. But I think feelings are the most important aspect and influencer of our behavior. We must feel our feelings!**
Feelings can be the most important aspect of any behavior model from one moment to the next. We're also intelligent, sentient beings who can and should manage our emotions (most of the time). The Echo-System minimizes feelings because this model aims to help people with long-term goal achievement and transformation.

---

[47] This is often termed a "premortem," and it's something I reviewed in *The Pressure Paradox* (2015).

Feelings are almost always tied to associated, underlying stories we narrate in our heads. Feelings are ephemeral – they tend to come and go. When we appreciate and understand the nature of our feelings, we can investigate the stories behind our emotions and modify, edit, and redirect them to create more optimistic, hopeful storylines.

8) How can I improve my self-image and self-esteem?
Start with the golden awareness that your self-image is a construct – something created over time that you can recreate. Identities are not etched in marble; they're pliable. When you recognize that your self-image is something you created, you gain permission to create a newer, better self-image that aligns with your goals and ideals.

Behaviors, habits, and skills tend to validate our beliefs about ourselves. Therefore, it's crucial to work on your behaviors, habits, and skills when working to reconstruct your self-image or improve your self-esteem. This is the Echo-System in action!

Tips for improving your self-image include:

- Test assumptions with small challenges. If you're highly critical of yourself, what top-of-mind story do you hear repeatedly? Challenge those stories and related labels.
- Change your self-talk. Denis E. Waitley, the author of *Psychology of Winning*, put it like this: "Relentless, repetitive self-talk is what changes our self-image."
- Follow the exercises in the previous chapter regarding script and story management.

9) How can I focus and concentrate better? I have ADD/ADHD. Can stories improve my focus?
First, emotions guide our focus. Thus, the emotion that supports concentration and focus is *harmony* – peace of mind.

Second, environmental factors consistently challenge our focus. Consider ways to make your environment more supportive of focus, such as turning off phone reminders, hiding other items on your computer screen, limiting social media, etc. For example, I have software that blacks out my screen when I write.

I recommend P.A.R.R. (Plan, Act, Record, Reassess) – The Habit Factor's habit-development methodology – to improve focus. P.A.R.R incorporates "focus periods" that have proven extremely helpful. In fact, The Habit Factor was born in many ways from my struggles with ADD/ADHD.

10) I know Who and What I want to become. Yet that character – person – doesn't feel real. Why?

It's not enough to think about and imagine who and what you want to become. The habits and skills that support your vision must exist – or at least be "under construction" – along with a supportive environment and narrative.

The good news is that when your narrative supports your targets, goals, and ideals, developing the right habits and skills becomes easier. It may take months or even years to become something and someone new – transformed.

11) I really struggle with habit tracking. Sometimes I can go for a couple of weeks and then lose track. How can I solve this and get better?

There is no failure when you keep putting in the effort. It's a "practice." In an example I've used throughout this book, Ben Franklin practiced habit tracking "on and off" for more than 60 years. Habit tracking is a long process – a lifetime endeavor. And a lifetime is lived one day at a time. Ultimately, tracking will help you develop and strengthen the habit of discipline, making tracking itself easier and more natural over time.

Some tips for habit tracking include:

- Understand your aversion stories relative to tracking. I once heard a peak performance coach insist that some personalities just can't or won't track. However, that's a story. With the right motivation, leverage, and supportive story, anyone can track.
- Know you can track *and* live your life. At an impressionable age, I once heard from a role model, "Life is to be lived, not tracked." I wish I hadn't! The truth is we can and should do both. Live and track! If it's important to you, track it!
- Understand that tracking is a reward. When we expect, believe, and know the reward is in the *process* (daily tracking) instead of a someday end goal, we'll experience heightened levels of control and happiness.
- Assess your desire. Many *say* they want to track yet lack the desire – a meaningful why story.
- Simplify your tracking system. Follow P.A.R.R. and choose only one or a few habits to track in the beginning.
- Ensure your environment is conducive to tracking. They don't call it "habitat" for nothing. Your environment has a powerful influence on your behavior, so create an environment favorable to tracking.
- Make your tracking sheet visible and accessible. Visibility dramatically facilitates the tracking process. I will sometimes tape my tracking sheet to my desk! Set up tracking reminders, and ask yourself what would make each habit easier to perform and track.

12) My purpose feels unreal and too large, way out of reach.

If your purpose doesn't feel achievable, begin with an imaginative narrative. Consider the following questions:

- What does your ideal outcome look like?
- What is required to create an ideal environment (resources, people, etc.)?
- Have you identified the necessary habits and skills?

- Are you tracking?
- What do your HERO script and storyline sound like?

Remind yourself that someone – likely far less capable than you – has already accomplished this or a similar goal.

13) I have a persistent level of doubt about my capabilities. This spurs negative emotions, frustration, and anger.

By assessing the validity of the doubt, you can address it head-on. It may be a valuable, critical warning advising that you must improve specific behaviors, skills, and habits. See the "Worries" chapter for a refresher.

14) I have underlying feelings of shame and guilt. How can I feel better?

To address underlying feelings of shame and guilt, do what you can to forgive yourself and acknowledge that the experience is in the past. Tell yourself you don't want a past experience to hold your present emotions hostage. Process your feelings of shame and guilt and use them to assess the lessons your experiences have taught you. (Review question 6.)

15) How long will it take to instill this discipline and ensure my stories, habits, and skills are aligned?

The time it takes depends on some key variables:

- Your desire and commitment to enact the behavior changes.
- Your commitment and resilience to repeat the supportive storylines.
- The goal itself will also significantly impact the timeline. Recall that Ryan Hall's transformation was a five-year endeavor.

16) How can I use character assimilation to help habit and skill development and foster new behaviors?

Every role or identity you accept – whether crafted intentionally or not – gives you a green light or red light for a specific behavior.

For example, a smoker identifies as a smoker. They'll say, "I'm a smoker." Some identify as "social smokers." This gives them permission – validation – to smoke with friends, when they drink, at parties, etc. They're crafting an identity that lets them validate a behavior.

There is an ideal character for every long-term goal and personal transformation. That ideal character behaves a certain way and has specific habits. Consider that "habitus" – the Latin root of the word habit – means "condition and/or character." Habits forge and constitute our character and thus direct and guide our behavior.

17) What is the mind!?

The mind is not a material, tangible thing. The mind is not the brain. The brain is in your skull – the mind is not.

I can only answer this question with intuition. Science has no explanation. Regrettably, too many "experts" write about the mind and brain as though they are interchangeable. Many bestsellers on topics about behavior and the brain never make this crucial distinction.

I attempted to tackle this esoteric-type question in *The Habit Factor*. I theorized that the mind is a compilation of the brain and heart energies. Further, the mind connects our consciousness and brain to an infinite storehouse of something that's been identified as the "super-conscious."

Curiously, I suspect it's when our subconscious operates around Alpha and Theta levels that it can "connect" to super-consciousness. This explains why creative insight strikes so often when we're doing habitual activities like brushing our teeth, showering, driving, jogging, or waking up.

18) How can I improve my HERO score?

Practice! Work on it – effort. Every day is a new day, a new battle. Recall Shay Eskew's HERO score is as close to 10 as it gets. Shay shared the following with me when I told him I wanted to use his story in this book: "One thing I cherish the most is being inducted into the National Wrestling Hall of Fame under the Medal of Courage designation. Only person from our 7x state championship team to be inducted (I was there for 3x of those). It meant the most because it had everything to do with mental commitment and being my best version of myself, not talent. I wasn't the best, but the award is based on those who live courageously and keep fighting."

19) When I look at the 3 Circles of Behavior Echo-System, I see how my environment is limiting some of the skills and habits I want to develop. My environment also feels toxic at times.

Being aware is the first step. Then, do what you can when you can to mitigate exposure to the negative aspects of your environment. At the same time, seek a supportive, conducive environment for new habits and skills.

Do your best not to let the environment overpower your HERO storylines as you move toward your goals and ideals.

20) I was recently promoted. My new role has me feeling inadequate.

Chances are excellent that whoever placed you in the new position believed in your skills, habits, and character.

The "inside" job for you may be appreciating your talents and skills and steering your inner scripts to support any new, required capabilities. At the same time, consciously foster new habits and skills to bolster your performance.

21) **When is the best time for script management? What is the process you recommend?**

As touched on in the "Art of Practice" and "Mastery" chapters, the key is exploring and experimenting persistently. I practice script management first thing in the morning.

Key script management habits to foster include meditation, journaling, and habit tracking. Developing a morning routine (which is just a series of habits) is very helpful.

22) **I feel completely overwhelmed. I've lost my job, and I'm going through a divorce. I'm unsure how this "story" stuff can help me.**

You must first ensure you're meeting your basic needs: food, water, shelter, etc. Seeking professional mental health or other support may be in order. Idealization and betterment initiatives are very tough to prioritize – and frankly, they shouldn't be.

Having said that, you should ensure your current stories help steer you in a favorable direction; running them through the HERO's checklist can be helpful.

Recognize that you're writing your end story *right now* with your present energy and thoughts. They will direct your emotions and behaviors and influence your environment.

No matter your situation, the 3 Circles of Behavior Echo-System is in effect and can be used as a guide or map toward an ideal future.

23) **I still don't see how tracking a few small habits will help me. Can you explain?**

Please reread the "Art of Practice" and "Mastery" chapters. Understand that small decisions and habits add up, and the longest journey begins with a single step. It's *now* that holds all the potential for the future you desire.

Furthermore, tracking provides essential data. Ryan Hall, the superhuman former elite marathoner, shared this with me: "I have always said that if you don't track training, how do you know if the training is working correctly? [You can] look back at training to try and identify what is causing the improvement or lack thereof. Not tracking is like performing science experiments and never writing anything down."

Sound familiar? You are exploring and experimenting. You need data! Plus, tracking reaffirms your commitment and intention.

24) I am very religious and take offense to the idea that religion is just a story. Can you explain?

Story, by definition, is both fact and fiction. There is no objective here to criticize religion. The key is to understand that religious stories are just that – stories. Further, these stories foster beliefs. Most religious people likely gain tremendous strength and value from their faith. At the same time, I've yet to meet anyone who has witnessed any of the biblical stories firsthand. That doesn't make them less valuable. It's simply labeling them what they are: *stories*.

25) I quit the habit of smoking instantly. I never needed to track any habits. Why?

First, congratulations!

The process of habit tracking aids habit formation. I say that tracking is required because most people aren't as committed. Habit tracking creates data that either reinforces the commitment or reveals it doesn't exist.

As I share in my presentations, if your story is extremely compelling, behavior change can be instant. For example, I knew a woman who smoked habitually. She explained, "No one knows what I've gone through," i.e., smoking helped her cope with an extremely difficult past. She insisted that quitting was out of the question. I saw her 18 months later; she was healthy, exercising, and taking care of herself. She admitted that she quit smoking and shared that she was three months pregnant.

It was obvious that her story about having a healthy baby and being a fit, healthy mother superseded her prior story: "I can't quit, and you don't know what I've been through!"

Our stories and related identities can be switched in an instant, impacting related behaviors and habits.

Important: While the changes in *identity* and *behavior* may be instantaneous, if either is not *practiced* with consistency – reinforced in the form of thought and behavior habits – former identities and related behaviors can reemerge. This is what is meant by performing daily practice (grabbing the "helm") more days than not.

26) By employing Joseph Campbell's quote to begin the "Meaning" chapter, you suggest we assign meaning to our lives. Why?

If you believe you're *destined* for a specific purpose, this is a story to which you've subscribed. It's something you believe deeply, whether it was created by you or for you. And belief is incredibly powerful and subtle.

27) It seems to me that our DNA and other inherent limitations are a major factor in achievement. I don't see that represented anywhere in the 3 Circles of Behavior Echo-System model.

Recall that the environment is both our *inputs* and *outputs*. The environment includes things that "happen to us" and things we can influence. Our DNA "happens" to us. As previously covered, the body – DNA – is represented as an environmental factor with significant influence on our emotions, feelings, behaviors, habits, and skills. Thus, our DNA impacts the goals and ideals we can achieve and experience.

28) **Is there a way to influence the placebo effect with any of this "stuff"? In other words, can I enhance a placebo by reinforcing a story I'm telling myself?**

This is a great question and one I'm probably not qualified to answer. Just like it's hard to tickle yourself, part of the magic of any placebo is that you have the expectation of a result, but at the same time, you're not supposed to be *aware* that what you're consuming isn't truly medicine. The idea of placebos, in many ways, validates – if only anecdotally – the ideas presented by the 3 Circles of behavior Echo-System. It demonstrates how our stories and thinking can influence our results (environment, of which the body is part).

29) **The terms "alignment" and "congruence" are used throughout, particularly as they apply to the 3 Circles of Behavior Echo-System. How does this fit with one's story? Can you provide an example?**

The scientific term I kept running across in my research was "SOC," or "Sense of Coherence." Coherence, by definition, includes both "logic and consistency." In short, a core theme within this book is to ensure that our most significant personal narratives are "aligned" – in *coherence* (consistent and logical) – with our goals and ideals. Alignment (dare I say) could be the "3 Cs of personal narrative" – a checklist for our most important stories. Are they *Congruent*, *Coherent*, and in *Concert* with your goals and ideals? There's probably another *3 Cs* book here!

Interestingly, SOC is considered an "adaptive *dispositional orientation*."[48] If there's an absence of coherence (logic and consistency), various issues may arise. Thus, psychology employs the concept of "SOC," which reflects someone's ability or inability to cope with life's stressors.[47]

---

[48] Recall the "Where?" chapter and emotional disposition.

A quick example, again, is the smoker who becomes pregnant and then quits smoking. This is coherence in action. She immediately *aligned* her narrative (matching the "3 Cs" above). Instantly, she adopted behaviors and habits in response to the *environmental stimulus* – her pregnancy.

30) You have no Ph.D. You are not a scientist. What makes you think you can write about this "stuff"?

Fair question. I'm writing about my experiences.

It's been over a decade since *The Habit Factor* was published. I received only one angry email from a Ph.D. (they never replied to my response) and one critical review via another Ph.D. who penned a conflicting thesis (book) – that pressure is "the enemy of success." In contrast, I've received countless "thank you" messages and appreciative comments from readers, including experts, behavioral scientists, and various Ph.Ds. and academics. Top universities have recommended and used *The Habit Factor*, and I've taught at various educational institutions.

Importantly, recent scientific studies on habit back *The Habit Factor's* original ideas relative to P.A.R.R. and how intention influences habit development as well as *habitstrength*. Some of these studies have emerged almost a decade *after The Habit Factor* was published.[48]

Numerous studies have already validated many of the ideas in this book. Further, this new behavior model, the 3 Circles of Behavior Echo-System," simply bundles all three works (*The Habit Factor, The Pressure Paradox,* and *Everything*), revealing how they work together to enhance one's effectiveness.

My intention is that this new behavior model makes behavior change more approachable and even easier to implement for those who are committed to their efforts. Additionally, teaching this model in coaching circles for nearly 18 months has further, if only anecdotally, validated its efficacy.

EPILOGUE

⚓

THERE'S MORE TO THE STORY

"There is no greater agony than bearing
an untold story inside you."
~Maya Angelou

In the interest of avoiding Maya's great agony (above), I
have borne this story and a handful of terrific "failures"
along with it.

Why share those stories? First, to demonstrate that
incongruency and incoherence between our narratives
(stories) and goals and ideals will result, at best, in mixed
results. Secondly, to demonstrate that, regardless of your
past, today's gift – *the present* – is your opportunity to get
your f*cking story straight.

Perhaps most importantly, I wanted to share the lessons
learned: how these experiences – combined with
experimentation and *meditation* – have guided me to this new
behavior model, the 3 Circles of Behavior Echo-System.
This model and framework have already shown an effective
way forward for many others.

EPILOGUE

***

As promised in the Preface, I will address the "F" bomb in the title.

I've been asked a handful of times, "Why ruin a perfectly good book with such offensive language?"

Here's the story.

First, please trust me when I tell you that settling on that title was a bit startling to me.

Startling and ironic.

Ironic because between the ages of 16-ish to 22, had you known me, you might've wondered if I knew any *other* words.

At the time, I likely would have justified my language choice by saying the F-word is just so practical and malleable.

A somewhat educational and entertaining video underscores this idea, describing the F-word as "the most versatile word in the English language." (It goes without saying, but I'll say it anyway: Adult language warning!)[49] At one point, the narrator demonstrates how the F-word can be nearly every word in a sentence. I'll let you figure out that sentence.

When my daughters were born, I challenged myself to rein in my language. I became semi-obsessed with ensuring they never heard me swear – not in front of them, anyway, and certainly not the F-word.[49]

Now, I finally get to share a Mia story (Eva's older sister).

Many of you will recall the spooky anecdote from *The Pressure Paradox* epilogue, where, at just four years old, Mia scratched out in crayon on a piece of paper "Metamorphisis = Die," then, "HrKLes." (Our dog Hercules had recently passed away).[50]

The incident was so bizarre that I'll share her scribbles one more time!

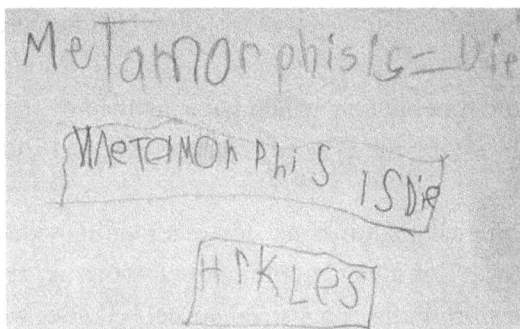

Back to Everything...

Mia was about 10 and had just been sent to her room because my wife heard her say the "F-word" for the very

---

[49] This alone is a semi-remarkable tribute to the "Art of Practice."
[50] For that entire story, see *The Pressure Paradox* epilogue.

first time! I was working at my desk nearby, observing the scene.

As Mia stomped her way up the stairs in protest, she stopped about halfway, tears in her eyes, red-faced and very upset. Looking at her mother pleadingly, she cried out, "Has dad ever said the F-word!?"

I was stunned.

I didn't know if I should laugh or cry.

At first, I was proud.

I'd done such a good job being aware of my language around my daughters that she was genuinely demanding to know if I'd ever used the F-word.

It was difficult for me to remain stoic.

Now, when I share that story with friends, I'll jokingly add that I yelled back (*which I did not do*):

"*F*ck yah! Are you f*cking kidding me!? I swear all the f*cking time!!*"

Apparently, it's a complicated relationship with the ol' F-bomb.

Having said that, the idea of using it within a title for my new book, particularly one about "right thought," was unfathomable!

Or was it?

I guess it all depends on the story I told myself.

So, here's a little more *backstory* regarding the title.

Initially, this project began even before I'd finished writing *The Pressure Paradox*; its working title was *Zen Psychology*, a domain name I registered in 2011. The domain hadn't been taken, and the two words together as a concept hadn't been formally used anywhere – no books, zero traceable references online. I rushed to purchase the domain. Today, there appear to be a few published works and references to Zen psychology. Nonetheless, I'd been sitting on the domain for years, just waiting for the right project to reveal itself.

While I liked the name *Zen Psychology* a lot, I *loved* the idea of Zen *as a practice of psychology*: a study of the practical application of its philosophy to produce an effective manner of behavior to achieve success, flow, or achievement (select the term that suits you best).

Then, about three-ish years ago, I awoke to the realization that *Zen Psychology* is not *this* book. Instead, *Zen Psychology* is the entire trilogy – the anthology – all three books combined.[50] Zen as a theme is laced across, around, and within all three books. It's even in the 3 C's of SuCCCess.

At that point, my mission was to align the new book's title with the flow and format of the previous two books, beginning with a *"The,"* as in, *The* Habit Factor and *The* Pressure Paradox. This first led me to *The Mind Refined*.

However, this title felt modest at best.

Despite years of effort, *The Mind Refined*, while fitting, was not going to serve the ultimate purpose of all these works:

- **To serve as many people as possible.**
- **To aid those who are ready, interested, and committed to authentic personal transformation and goal achievement.**

In this insanely competitive, microwave, TikTok, two-second attention span world, *Everything* isn't just competing with books; it's competing with <u>EVERYTHING</u>*!*

We asked, would *The Mind Refined* help us best achieve that purpose?

Despite knowing that there was plenty of value behind the cover to support the book's ongoing success and longevity, the unavoidable reality is that people must notice the book *first*.

A buddy's fiancé confessed the following as I shared my deliberation story between the two very different titles.

"Oh!" She practically yelled as she pointed. "*That* title is far more interesting!"

END OF STORY.
(For now…)

INVICTUS

Invictus

BY WILLIAM ERNEST HENLEY

Out of the night that covers me,
Black as the pit from pole to pole,
I thank whatever gods may be
For my unconquerable soul.

In the fell clutch of circumstance
I have not winced nor cried aloud.
Under the bludgeonings of chance
My head is bloody, but unbowed.

Beyond this place of wrath and tears
Looms but the Horror of the shade,
And yet the menace of the years
Finds and shall find me unafraid.

It matters not how strait the gate,
How charged with punishments the scroll,
I am the master of my fate,
I am the captain of my soul.

ABOUT THE AUTHOR

Martin Grunburg is the creator/inventor of The Habit Factor app and the author of the international bestselling book sharing the same name. He's widely regarded as the father of the modern habit-tracking movement, originally publishing The Habit Factor app in 2009 – the first app to provide a unique and simplified goal achievement methodology specifically via positive habit development and alignment.

Martin presented these revolutionary insights about habit and goal achievement at TEDx in the United Arab Emirates in 2010. His work has been featured in the world's most popular productivity blogs, such as Lifehacker.com and Mashable.com, as well as The New York Times, C|Net, and OpenForum.

Martin has been nominated twice for the Entrepreneur of the Year award and has twice led his team to win the Better Business Bureau Torch Award for Marketplace Ethics.

Martin served on the board of Big Brothers Big Sisters regionally in San Diego for 10 years and became a Big Brother in 1999. He served on the Entrepreneurs Organization (San Diego) board as the Mentor Chair for two years. Before that, he served as a volunteer instructor for Junior Achievement, teaching "Success Skills" to some of the city's more economically challenged high schools.

Martin is an avid waterman, surfer, and sailor who has completed the Catalina Classic (a 32-mile open-ocean paddle) multiple times. He considers himself an "accidental triathlete," having completed several full Ironman-distance triathlons (one in France). Martin resides in Pacific Beach, California, with his legendary wife, world-class editor, sage, and saint, Gretchen.
***

Behavior Change Professionals & Coaches: Learn to teach **P.A.R.R.** and the **3 Circles of Behavior Echo-System**. Collaborate and share best practices with other professionals. Become a Certified Professional today; learn more here: https://certified.thehabitfactor.com.

For all professional, corporate, and non-profit speaking and workshop inquiries: Please visit: http://thehabitfactor.com/meet-martin.

Readers: Please keep sharing your success stories surrounding *The Habit Factor*, *The Pressure Paradox*, and now, *EVERYTHING*. Email: success (at) thehabitfactor.com.

BONUSES

Thank you for reading! I hope you enjoyed the book! If
you've received value, please share it with your friends and loved
ones. **Also, please review the book while it's fresh and you're
here! This QR code is a quick, *direct* link to the book's
review page on Amazon**. No scrolling or searching! Scan this
QR code, and you'll be done in two minutes. Thank you!

Instant Amazon review link for EVERYTHING. Thank you!

If you write a review, please share it at our website (URL below) to
access either a live or recorded Q&A about the book. Additionally,
there are new guides and additional information we couldn't fit into this
book. There's even an omitted chapter and bonus audio. Please visit:
everythingastory.com.

How-to guides to put *EVERYTHING* into practice:
- The How-to Guide for Millennials and Gen Zers
- The How-to Guide for Entrepreneurs, Executives, and Managers
- The How-to Guide, Mantras and Meditations
- Bonus Audio (not on Audible)
- Live or recorded webinar Q&A about the book with me

Begin your personal transformation journey now!
"EVERYTHING" readers also save on our Automatic Goals and
VIP coaching courses. Just email: AGVIP@equilibrium-ent.com
with the subject line: *Everything AG Discount!*

Subscribe to the top-ranked "**Habits 2 Goals**" Podcast: iTunes or Android.

ACKNOWLEDGMENTS

*"There are two great days in your life: the day you're
born, and the day you find out why."*
~Mark Twain

There are far too many people to thank individually. Having said that, I feel compelled to make an effort, starting at home with Gretchen, my wife, the one who makes sense of this "stuff." Twenty-four years married and counting. As I write this, it's our anniversary. Your beauty and greatness inspire me to be better. To my daughters Mia and Eva, who provide wonderful anecdotes (dare I say *stories*) and continue to impress and inspire me – thank you, girls. Love you! My parents – this work is dedicated to you both. You have always done your best to ensure I was crafting hero-like stories.

Keeping it in the family: Big bro…there's no doubt that because of you, I started surfing. To RG, as stated, a legendary brother. I didn't know *that* story was going to emerge as it did. Thank you! Thank you to Denise and the heroic nephews, Luke, Noah, and Julius. To the in-laws, Bapop (among the world's greatest storytellers) and Nanny, always incredibly supportive, as are the bro-in-law John, sister-in-law Lisa, and my favorite, phenomenally bright and athletic nieces Lindsey and Lily. To Grandma Margaret and Uncle Sean, you are sorely missed and never forgotten. To my hall-of-fame-HERO "little" bro Mark! One day at a time! To the Oliver crew: Roxy, Chloe (the rat dog), Tinky, and Hobie!

I'd like to thank myself – my former self ;). Without the handful of confusing and conflicting stories I carried, this work wouldn't exist. Speaking of work, thanks to Professor Mark Turner and his profound work, which has been instrumental.

To Rick Sessinghaus, one of the world's great coaches (I'm supposed to say golf coaches, but anyone who understands "coaching" and "golf" knows that each transcends its respective fields). Thank you, Rick, for a phenomenal Foreword – it's so fitting to have our backstory *tee up* this book a decade later!

To Dr. Peter Chee, who told me via LinkedIn back in 2016 when we officially "met" that he had studied my work and "gained valuable learning from it." In early 2021, I was eager to send him the excerpt. A couple of months went by, and I'd heard nothing. Then, in early May, he sent me a terrific endorsement requesting and encouraging me (despite the book not yet being completed) to begin teaching its lessons to his "Certified Chief Master Coaches."

To executive and leadership coach Timi Gleason, who jumped on the same early excerpt. A phenomenal executive coach with her own incredibly genius and creative spin on coaching. Timi's another longtime Certified Habit Factor Professional. Be sure to check her out at https://soulworkmaps.com.[51]

To the various podcasts and their hosts who've interviewed me to talk about habits, goals, and pressure! In particular, Andrew Ferebee, Aidan McCullen, Brian Conroy, Luke DePron, Jeremy Pound, Jim Beach, Phoebe Chongchua, and Donna Maria.

To Brian Tracy, EB, and company – it's a phenomenal honor to have BT's support and endorsement behind all three works in the trilogy.

To Jen Grant! Our legendary ambassador of client experience at The Habit Factor and her great insight into the Pain-Regret Chart! To Anna Laden, who's taken our social media efforts to new heights – and it's only the beginning! Speaking of Ladens, thank you, Chris, the master programmer behind habit.us (beta). To another Chris, Christopher John Payne, thanks so much for the friendship also birthed by THF. (BTW, I'm still processing your 106 pages of notes! Most were corrected.) Thank you for a decade-plus of support! It's fun to look back and see where and how this all began with THF.

To the notable personalities, business leaders, and thought leaders who continue to endorse and recommend my work: Verne Harnish, John Assaraf, Holly Green, Professor Glenn Fox, Jack Daly, Mark Moses, Tony Lillios, Jairek Robbins, Kevin Daum, David Katz, and Cameron Herold. To Jack Daly, in particular: As I've always said, Sir, you *are* THF epitomized, and, not coincidentally, we met because of that book! Thanks for the continued inspiration and demonstrating how anyone can and should live a life by design!

To the HEROes and dear friends I cite in this book: Rosalind Savage, Klyn Elsbury, Shay Eskew, John Stein, and of course, Felipe! Ted Ryce, your insightful commentary in our H2G interview has been spectacular color and support for the 3 Circles of Behavior Echo-System. And your personal story continues to inspire.

Ryan Hall, thanks for sharing your inspiring personal transformation story and insights and answering my questions! Check out Ryan and Jay's run coaching site: https://www.runfreetraining.com/. To Gary M. and Stephanie W., thank you for thinking of THF/MG. This is an exciting journey and new venture! To Cathey Fisher, Laura Stephens Robel, and the other stalwarts in The Habit Factor communities. Thanks to the EVERYTHING launch group and various early supporters and reviewers of the early excerpt: S. Boren, April S., and Bennett F. A massive thank you to the scores of entrepreneurs and business

ACKNOWLEDGMENTS

leaders who've encouraged me over the years and who endorse and recommend my works: Michele K., Michael A., Greg G., Drew G.; Jeremy P., Joe A., Scott P., Michael E., Ian O., Eileen A.J., R. Whyte, Brian M., Ramos 2x, and so many others…*advance apologies to those I've missed!*

To Martha K. Cullimore and the Kling clan! Forever grateful, Martha, for your early support of THF! To Ron Harrell, another legendary business coach and CPP who let me bounce many of these ideas off him. Control does exist ;).

To David Allen (Rockersan) for the continued insightful anecdotes and perspectives. Your assistance with the exercises early on was massive! Thank you! To Ray Drasnin for working your magic and taking the time to understand the message, model, and value to readers for years to come.

To all past and present AG and Unstuck participants! *Keep on trackin'!*

To Dani and Anna of dna photo + style, thank you for the excellent photos. Dani, stay after it – you're onto something great with your writing! Speaking of photographers and videographers, Coco – for nearly a decade, you've been chasing me from one event to another. Plus, you're a surf and nature photographer par excellence. To Nanci and Greg, Mary and John: We miss our old neighbors!

To the legendary 4T IT team: AA, GC, SM, MR, and DW. To witness your daily teamwork, personal growth, and exceptional service is perpetually inspiring!

To the men aboard the Indies trader III: I had no idea that trip would come into play…in a few different ways. An epic adventure, and the surf didn't suck either. And, to the Mayor – Drew Boyles. Love getting your messages and emails, updates on tracking, and continued kind comments and referrals relative to THF. It was fun sharing an early version of this book's WHEN chapter with you. Worth remembering: "Today is the 8th day of the month; tomorrow is the 13th." To Eric N., it was an honor to meet you on that trip! I'm still floored by your kindness and surprise reading and review of THF! Many people buy a book; few read it, and fewer still review it. THANK YOU!

To Paul Palmer, you are missed. It's important to have heroes. You were a hero to many and likely the best leader I'd ever known. You will not be forgotten. To Matt Belshin for the serendipitous near collision in the hallway, only to find out you'd just given your elite athlete son THF! Greatly appreciate your insights and support.

To the many notable resources and works presented throughout the book, in the footnotes and endnotes, including various Ted talks. To Brian Tracy (again): You probably have nearly a half-dozen great quotes scattered throughout this work, but your lifetime of work and lessons permeate throughout. Other notable personal development greats, past and present:

EVERYTHING Is A F*cking Story

Victor Frankl and his *Man's Search for meaning*, Maxwell Maltz and his *Psycho-Cybernetics*, and BT's *Psychology of Achievement*. Additionally, Tony Robbins, Dr. Stephen Covey, Napoleon Hill, Norman Vincent Peale, Warren S. Rustand, Michael Gerber, Darren Hardy, Tony Smith (in memoriam – an all-time leader, entrepreneur, philanthropist, and great advocate of THF), Gary Ridge, Denis E. Waitley, Martin Seligman, and David J. Schwartz.

To the philosophical masters who've made writing and learning enjoyable: Kurt Vonnegut (he'd laugh at this company), Lao Tzu, Confucius, Aristotle, Socrates, Marcus Aurelius, Henry David Thoreau, Ralph Waldo Emerson, Seneca, Epictetus, Pythagoras, Alan Watts, and Jim Rohn (to name a small handful). To the great American hero and perhaps a great-grandfather of personal development, Benjamin Franklin. Collectively, these authors and thinkers have likely saved me from myself countless times.

To my former, retired partners, a distinct thank you: Edmon, Christine, Duke, and Colleen. (Colleen, you will never be forgotten. You were as beautiful as you were creative. You are missed dearly!)

To the CIC gang from way back in the day, especially our fearless leader Greg Schneider (long live the legend!) and Leonard Loo. To Felipe (again) for all the memories and epic stories. To the "BAND," where it all began: Jed, Billy, and Scotty! Say it one more time, Scotty: "We were great in the '80s!" To the Friday Golf crew: Al, G-Man, Rockersan, and the "occasionals," Billy, Halvin, and Ron. To Goldie Mathews for purchasing "Any Party," a painting from my early days, reminding and encouraging me that it's time to start creating more art! To Bing B., your boundless support for THF and aiding in our informal "habit study" in China is unforgettable!

To the scores of incredible personal and corporate sponsors over the years (in no particular order): ITD World, IREM, SENTRE Partners (Williams & Spathas and Co.), Bird Rock Systems, Zenzi, College Works, Dolce & Pane, Signature Furniture Rental, Entrepreneurs Organization, Vistage (Mr. Chalmers), Big Brothers Big Sisters San Diego, SAGE Executive Group (Rollins & Yui), TEDx Al Ain, San Diego Professional Coaches Alliance, Sales Leadership Alliance, Southwest Realtors Association, NAI, JMS/SPAWAR, U.S. Green Chamber, EO, EO Accelerator, The Rock! Hardwick, Hayes, Carder, Preston, Reynolds, Levy, Moaddeli, Ortiz, Case, Wilf, Messac, Wright, Sergio, and Berman (again). Plus, old-school Rock: Alger, Baggerly, Bertone, Carr, Hoffman, Levy, and Steel. Finally, R2, Hayes, Stein, Foster, and Noe. *Keep on trackin' and Stay after it!*

To our past, present, and future Certified Professionals. The best is yet to come! *I'm out of space; to those I've failed to mention, I will get you next time!* ~mg

NOTES

EVERYTHING Is A F*cking Story

NOTES

ENDNOTES

Bibliography and Additional References

[1] Grunburg, Martin. *The Habit Factor*, Equilibrium Enterprises (November 11, 2010):
https://www.amazon.com/Habit-Factor-Innovative-Achieve-Success/dp/0982050178

[2] See this National Library of Medicine study on regrets:
https://www.ncbi.nlm.nih.gov/pmc/articles/PMC2394712/

[3] See more on "thought worms" in this Nature Communications article:
https://www.nature.com/articles/s41467-020-17255-9

[4] See the triangles and circle video on YouTube:
https://www.youtube.com/watch?v=VTNmLt7QX8E

[5] Turner, Mark. *The Literary Mind: The Origins of Thought and Language*, Revised ed. Edition, Oxford University Press (December 17, 1998):
https://www.amazon.com/Literary-Mind-Origins-Thought-Language-ebook/dp/B004WN4WIC/

[6] Gottschall, Jonathan. *The Storytelling Animal: How Stories Make Us Human*, Mariner Books (April 10, 2012):
https://www.amazon.com/Storytelling-Animal-Stories-Make-Human-ebook/dp/B005LVR6BQ

[7] Visit YouTube for examples of compression, metaphor, and metonymy action:
https://www.youtube.com/watch?v=kiHw3N6d1Js

[8] NPR: "Can You Tell Your Life Story in Exactly Six Words?":
https://www.npr.org/2010/02/03/123289019/can-you-tell-your-life-story-in-exactly-six-words

ENDNOTES

---

[9] The Atlantic, "Masters of Love":
https://www.theatlantic.com/health/archive/2014/06/happily-ever-after/372573/

[10] Merriam-Webster definition of story:
https://www.merriam-webster.com/dictionary/story

[11] Behavior change models are largely relative to societal health norms and initiatives. See "Behavioral Change Models":
https://www.ncbi.nlm.nih.gov/pmc/articles/PMC3940013/
https://sphweb.bumc.bu.edu/otlt/mph-modules/sb/behavioralchangetheories/BehavioralChangeTheories_print.html

[12] Juvenal: "Never does Nature say one thing and Wisdom another." For more context on pressure and growth, see the Viktor Frankl interview, "Youngsters need challenges," on YouTube:
https://www.youtube.com/watch?v=ImonPWt7VOA

[13] As explained in my TEDx presentation, this was a process to minimize regrets in my life. Jeff Bezos shared his experience doing the same thing, calling it a "regret minimization framework":
https://www.youtube.com/watch?v=jwG_qR6XmDQ

[14] Learn about habit development and alignment following P.A.R.R.:
https://thehabitfactor.com/templates

[15] See this Hero's Journey comparative infographic for a clearer understanding:
https://venngage.com/blog/heros-journey/

[16] See more of George Lucas's comments on Joseph Campbell:
http://www.comiccollectorlive.com/forum/default.aspx?g=posts&t=22905#:

[17] Hero's Journey, Wikipedia: Public Domain, Creative Commons:
https://commons.wikimedia.org/wiki/File:Heroesjourney.svg#filelinks

[18] Joe Rogan Experience: Clip from Moonshot podcast: "Live your life like a documentary crew is following you around":
https://www.youtube.com/watch?v=YwD_gt1RSQI

[19] The study was published in the April issue of the journal *Emotion*. Gilovich's co-author was Shai Davidai, Ph.D. '15 of The New School for Social Research. Read more at this Cornell article:
https://as.cornell.edu/news/woulda-coulda-shoulda-haunting-regret-failing-our-ideal-selves

[20] Bates, Alex. *Augmented Mind: AI, Humans and the Superhuman Revolution*, published April 2019:
https://www.amazon.com/gp/product/1732854815/

[21] Our discussion about AI and neural networks leads us to a powerful correlation: Pattern learning is intended for goal-directed behavior. Check out the Habits 2 Goals podcast for more:
https://podcasts.apple.com/us/podcast/habits-2-goals-habit-factor-podcast-martin-grunburg/id953300407

[22] Grunburg, Martin. *The Pressure Paradox*, Equilibrium Enterprises; 1st edition (October 17, 2015):
https://www.amazon.com/Pressure-ParadoxTM-Maximum-Productivity-Performance-ebook/dp/B016WLQUCC/

[23] Steel, Mitch W., *The 3 C's of Success*, Equilibrium Enterprises (October 1, 1998):
https://www.amazon.com/Cs-SUCCCESS-Mitch-W-Steel/dp/0982050100

[24] The Tim Ferriss Show #427: Michael Lewis on the Crafts of Writing, Friendship, Coaching, Happiness, and More:
https://www.youtube.com/watch?v=L5qWV1EG0Rc

ENDNOTES

---

[25] Herman, Todd, *The Alter Ego Effect*, Harper Business, illustrated edition (February 5, 2019):
https://www.amazon.com/Alter-Ego-Effect-Identities-Transform-ebook/dp/B075WPWMSK

[26] One example can be found in this study (note "coherence" and "optimism"):
https://www.tandfonline.com/doi/full/10.1080/23311886.2018.1489458

[27] Isaacson, Walter, *Benjamin Franklin, An American Life*, Simon & Schuster (June 1, 2004):
https://www.amazon.com/Benjamin-Franklin-American-Walter-Isaacson/dp/074325807X

[28] Franklin, Benjamin, *The Autobiography of Benjamin Franklin*, Project Gutenberg:
https://www.gutenberg.org/files/20203/20203-h/20203-h.htm

[29] Maslow Hierarchy of Needs, Wikipedia, attribution, Lord Belbury:
https://commons.wikimedia.org/wiki/File:Maslow%27s_Hierarchy_of_Needs2.svg#file

[30] Duckworth, Angela. *Grit*, Scribner, 1st edition (May 3, 2016):
https://www.amazon.com/Grit-Passion-Perseverance-Angela-Duckworth/dp/1501111108

[31] View Simon Sinek's Ted Talk:
https://www.ted.com/talks/simon_sinek_how_great_leaders_inspire_action?language=en

[32] For more on this, see Adam Grant's Ted Talk, "The Surprising Habits of Original Thinkers":
https://www.youtube.com/watch?v=fxbCHn6gE3U

[33] Image: Festina Lente: Arminiuzz, CC BY 3.0, Creative Commons license via Wikimedia Commons:
https://en.wikipedia.org/wiki/Festina_lente

[34] John Wooden's Pyramid of Success:
https://www.thewoodeneffect.com/pyramid-of-success/

[35] See *Men's Journal*'s article on Ryan Hall to learn more about his transformation:
https://www.mensjournal.com/health-fitness/marathoner-ryan-hall-transformation/

[36] Find more info on Ryan Hall and Jay Stephenson's training program at the Run Free Training website:
https://runfreetraining.com/

[37] For a master lesson on responding, watch this YouTube video on Nick Vujicic:
https://www.youtube.com/watch?v=zOzsjEmjjHs

[38] Ryan Hall's Instagram STORY is titled "Transformation!" True Story!
https://www.instagram.com/stories/highlights/18164951356044822/?hl=en

[39] Read this *Queen's Gazette* article for more on thought worms:
https://www.queensu.ca/gazette/stories/discovery-thought-worms-opens-window-mind

[40] Free versions exist for both the Habit Factor iOS app and Android app:
iOS: https://apps.apple.com/us/app/the-habit-factor-lite/id324002311
Android:
https://play.google.com/store/apps/details?id=com.habitfactorlite

ENDNOTES

---

⁴¹ Learn about qualifying to become a Habit Factor Certified
Professional:
https://certified.thehabitfactor.com/

⁴² Read more about studies on the health benefits of forming a narrative
on the American Psychological Association website and National
Library of Medicine website:
https://www.apa.org/monitor/jun02/writing
https://pubmed.ncbi.nlm.nih.gov/11045774/

⁴³ Learn more about the benefits of self-efficacy from the International
Journal of Research Culture Society and the International Journal of
School and Cognitive Psychology:
http://ijrcs.org/wp-content/uploads/201804075.pdf
https://www.longdom.org/open-access-pdfs/prediction-of-happiness-
based-on-selfregulation-and-selfefficacy-among-female-students-of-
secondary-highschools-in-hamedan-2469-9837-1000217.pdf

⁴⁴ The NASA website explains more about waves and points:
https://earthobservatory.nasa.gov/images/149605/worlds-longest-
wave#

⁴⁵ Exercise is from the HabitXP Planner:
https://shop.thehabitfactor.com

⁴⁶ Learn more about the Four Stages of Competence:
https://en.wikipedia.org/wiki/Four_stages_of_competence

⁴⁷ More on Sense of Coherence:
https://www.sciencedirect.com/topics/medicine-and-dentistry/sense-
of-coherence

⁴⁸ Does habit weaken the relationship between intention and behavior?
Revisiting the habit-intention interaction hypothesis:
https://compass.onlinelibrary.wiley.com/doi/full/10.1111/spc3.12553

---

[49] The F-word. Language warning: Educational and entertaining YouTube video regarding the F word's versatility: https://youtu.be/cxpV8D8K9JI

[50] For those interested in Zen Psychology and my other upcoming courses, check out Automatic Goals: https://automaticgoals.com

[51] Visit Timi Gleason's ingenious Soulwork Maps creation: https://soulworkmaps.com

www.ingramcontent.com/pod-product-compliance
Lightning Source LLC
Chambersburg PA
CBHW020603270326
41927CB00005B/153